ADVANCE PRAISE

"Exhaustively researched and movingly written" - **Jonathan Gornall**

Eighty years on from the start of the genocidal calamity that claimed the lives of six million Jews in Europe, there is a danger that, as the voices of the last survivors can be heard no more, the true meaning of the Holocaust will be lost to history.

The House on Thrömerstrasse, an exhaustively researched and movingly written book, serves the vital purpose of keeping alive that meaning, not through a broad retelling of the horror story that is the Holocaust, but by immersing the reader in the lives of the Böhm family and their descendants.

After all, while history can be too vast to grasp, each of us has a mother and a father and the story of the Böhms – one more ordinary family striving to make its way in the world, just like our own, until the rise of Nazism blotted out its sun – is one with which we can all identify.

Author Ron Vincent's achievement is to flesh out the story of the lives and times of this family with just enough detail to bring to life its hopes, dreams and sufferings without bogging down the narrative with minutiae – a trap into which many writers of nonfiction, determined to deploy all the fruits of their prodigious research, frequently fall.

Vincent also manages to maintain the emotional distance from his subject demanded of any narrator seeking credibility. This is an even more impressive achievement given that he is the son of Ruth Böhm, who fled from Germany to England in 1939, and the great-grandson of Louis Böhm, the draper from Katscher (today Kietrz in Poland), whose story opens the book and ends in tragedy.

Tragedy is, of course, a theme that runs through this book, but all is not darkness. Vincent is determined to demonstrate that the human spirit can endure and rise above the darkest of days, which he does by following the dispersed footsteps of a family that emerges from the chaos of the Second World War to forge new beginnings in Australia, South America, the United States and the United Kingdom.

There will be some, of course, who question the need for yet another book about the Holocaust and its victims. That such reminders are necessary, however, is depressingly evident in the resurgence of antisemitism in the nationalist narratives of far-right groups across Europe – including, of all places, in Germany.

Speaking in September 2020 at the 70th anniversary of the Central Council of Jews in Germany, German Chancellor Angela Merkel pointed to the rise of antisemitic conspiracy theories and hate speech on social media and spoke of her shame that "many Jews do not feel safe, do not feel respected in our country".

It is for them, and for the millions of Jews who passed this way before, that books such as *The House on Thrömerstrasse* must be written.

Jonathan Gornall is a British author and journalist, formerly with *The Times*. His book *How To Build A Boat – A Father, His Daughter and The Unsailed Sea* is published by Simon & Schuster in the UK and by Scribner in the US.

When I first opened this book my heart sank. Although I too am fascinated by my own European family history the idea of reading a long-winded description of another family's journey of sorrow, terror and survival was not greatly appealing but I was willing to have a look at it. As the author started to describe how he had pieced together so much of their story in beautifully coherent and elegant prose I felt encouraged. Here was obsession and integrity combined in this relatively short investigation of his mother Ruth Böhm's family background in an attempt to come to terms with her life and indeed his own.

Having visited the sites of their homes and businesses in Upper Silesia he has brought them to life in words and pictures and then set them in the context of the political and social upheavals of the early 20th century and the Second World War. Katscher, Breslau and other towns of culture and cultivation that were laid waste by the Germans and then the Russians have become real places for me, however much their names have now changed as they were rebuilt in what became Poland. Just as the grimness became hard to bear he flashes to the huge and thriving family that exists all over the world now and one is left with hope and light. Having been born in Wales and studied German, he too had lived in Australia where the majority of the family had regrouped and revived their fortunes so you have a real flavour of their new lives rather than an academic gathering of notes, an understanding of his own discovery of his Jewish identity. His present life in Germany turns the wheel onwards.

What I hadn't realised that I would find was more information about my own father's background. His journey started in Vienna, going via Dachau, Kitchener Camp in Kent and the Pioneer Corps. I found myself looking closely at the photos just in case he was there in the background. Of course it was unlikely but he would have shared so much with those who were there. This and the political commentary put the book on a new footing for me. Someone has done valuable research on my behalf and I believe many more families who escaped Nazi persecution. This may be a very personal book but it is a shaft of light that I hadn't found elsewhere and a rewarding read.

Kathy Shock is an active member of the Oxford Jewish community. Her own father left Vienna via Dachau, then fought in the British army after a period in Kitchener Camp Pioneer Corps and met her Jewish English mother in London. He managed to bring his own parents over to the UK on a domestic visa just in time and most of her family were dispersed across the world, rather than perishing in the Holocaust. But her roots and their journeys are similar to those of the author, as are those of countless Jews spread worldwide.

The House on Thrömerstrasse is a very readable account of the author's personal journey into uncovering his true identity. When he discovers that his mother was Jewish, he embarks upon a fascinating journey into the past which leads him from the Isle of Man, where his mother was interned, to the house of his great grandparents in Upper Silesia.

Tina Delavre is Honorary Vice President of B'nai B'rith, Frankfurt and Editor of the Jewish Immigrants Journal 'Unsere Stimme'.

Ron Vincent's book travels through time. His story spans 150 years and shares an engrossing family tale of tragedy, survival and renewal. But at its heart, this is a man's quest for identity and belonging which he ultimately finds in his maternal lineage to the Bohm family.

There is much to discover when reading this book – the sadness and bravery of the individuals who survived but ultimately the intimacy in the rich fabric of family which is something the Holocaust could not destroy. Yes, the Holocaust left its scars and wounds but it also built resilience and gave the Bohm family new beginnings in far-off lands, which is something that may never have been deemed possible or even imaginable to Louis and Jenni Bohm. Their legacy lives on in this book.

Dr Leah Kaye is an experienced management consultant and academic with over 30 years experience in higher education, organisational training and management education.

The House on Thrömerstrasse is one of those wonderful examples of a real-life history that touches the heart and educates the mind simultaneously. It reinforces how important memoirs, biographies and family stories are as they provide a source of information which can be quite unique. They reflect individual experiences and attitudes that could in time become priceless, archival material. [...] We are losing, or have lost, many of our World War II survivors. Many of those survivors did not write their stories so we have lost them forever. But where they did share their stories with children and grandchildren, it is now up to those children and grandchildren to document these rich, powerful, important stories or more will become extinct. Ron Vincent is to be congratulated. He managed to cleverly integrate the right amount of family history with what was happening during the most vile dictatorship in world history and saved his family story from slipping into oblivion. It is a heartfelt example of the indomitable and unbreakable human survival instinct with all the twists and turns of the author's family's wins and losses. An inspiring and satisfying adventure. We will remember the Böhm Family.

Annette Janic, first generation Australian who arrived in Australia under the International Refugee Organization (IRO) following World War II., and author of *War Child, Survival Betrayal Secrets*.

THE HOUSE ON THRÖMERSTRASSE

A STORY OF REBIRTH AND RENEWAL IN THE WAKE OF THE HOLOCAUST

RON VINCENT

ap

ISBN 9789493231313 (ebook)

ISBN 9789493231306 (paperback)

ISBN 9789493231320 (hardcover)

ISBN 9789493231375 (audiobook)

Publisher: Amsterdam Publishers The Netherlands

info@amsterdampublishers.com

The House on Thrömerstrasse is part of the series Holocaust Survivor True Stories WWII

Copyright © Ron Vincent 2021

German edition: *Das Haus in der Thrömerstrasse: Eine Geschichte von Wiedergeburt und Erneuerung nach dem Holocaust*, Amsterdam Publishers, 2021

Cover image: The House on Thrömerstrasse, c. 1935

All Rights Reserved. No part of this publication may be reproduced or transmitted in any form or by any means, electronic or mechanical, including photocopy, recording or any other information storage and retrieval system, without prior permission in writing from the publisher.

CONTENTS

Advance Praise	1
Böhm Family Tree	13
Prologue	17

PART I
The Beginnings of a Dynasty	31
The Gathering Storm	48
Escape and Internment	56
Tragedy and Despair	85
Peace at Last and a New Life	99
Sanctuary and Renewal	105

PART II
The Shattering of a Silesian Dream	117
The Siege of Breslau	124
The Fall of Katscher and Gleiwitz	131
A Land Transformed	135

PART III
Katscher's Dark History	143
Retracing the Steps	155
A Surprising Discovery	177

Epilogue	185
Acknowledgments	207
References	209
Amsterdam Publishers Holocaust Library	211

Dedicated to the memory of

Louis Böhm

and his son Siegbert

and daughter-in-law Clara

who perished in the Holocaust

BÖHM FAMILY TREE

In the family trees, the anglicized names were used for family members rather than the German names that they were born with: George/Georg; Kate/Käthe; Henry/Heinrich; Gary/Gerd; Walter/Walther; Arthur/Artur.

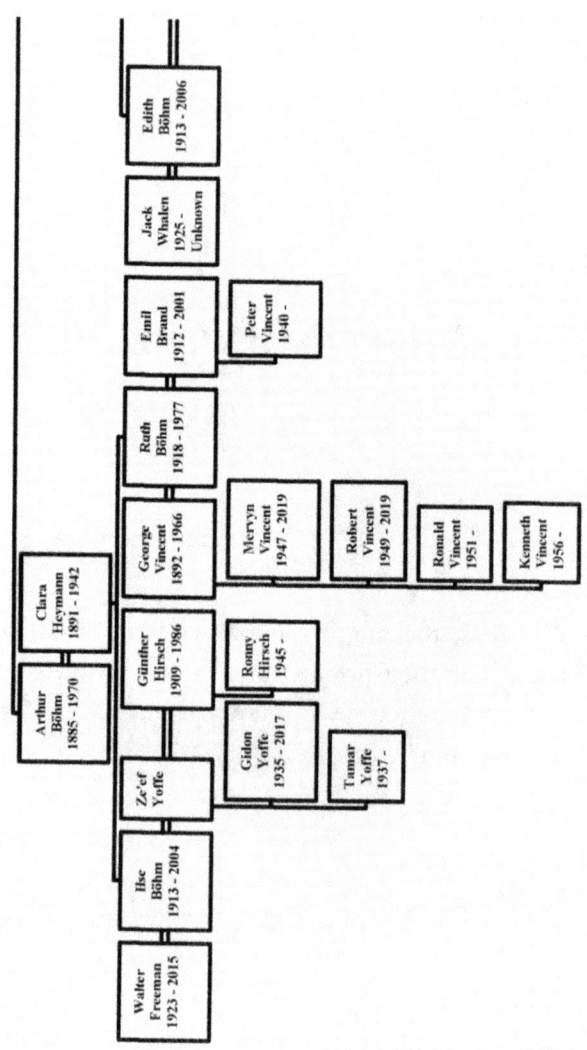

Family Tree Louis and Jenni Böhm

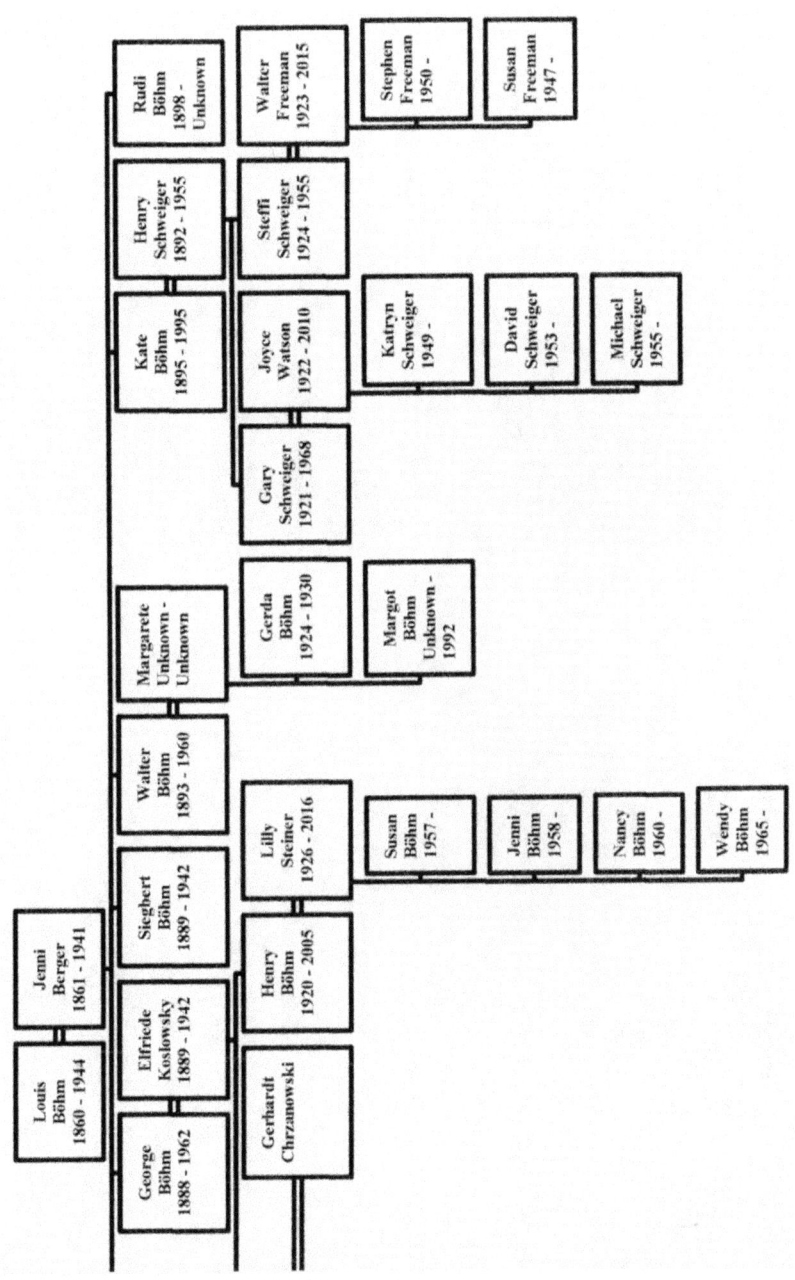

Family Tree: First Four Generations

PROLOGUE

On 21 May 1939, with suitcase in hand, Ruth Böhm walked into the crowded ticket hall of Breslau central railway station, no doubt accompanied by her mother, Clara, and other members of the family. Her final destination was to be a modest detached house in a quiet, leafy street in Abbots Langley, England, where she was to take up a position as a domestic help working for the Sadler family that consisted of two elderly spinsters, their widowed brother and a young teenage girl. She was leaving Germany because she was Jewish and, since Hitler had come to power in 1933, everyday life for Jewish people had become almost unbearable and, in many cases, increasingly dangerous.

Shortly after being elected chancellor, Hitler introduced the Nüremberg Race Laws, which were designed to strip Jews of their German citizenship, basic human rights and freedom of movement. This effectively made it impossible for them to work in public positions, enjoy the same freedoms as non-Jewish citizens did or indeed lead anything approaching a normal life.

Anti-Jewish feeling, which had been simmering beneath the surface for generations, spread quickly throughout Germany over the next few years. This growing resentment quickly turned to hate that finally erupted on 9 November 1938, the so-called Kristallnacht, when hundreds of Jewish synagogues and businesses were burnt to the ground and reduced to ashes.

As a result, Jewish people could no longer feel safe in Germany and many parents in particular resolved to do everything within their power to ensure that their children and younger members of the family could be sent to another country where they would be able to make a fresh start in peace and not be persecuted simply because they belonged to the wrong race. This could not have been a happy occasion for the members of the Böhm family who were present at the station on that day. Never having been away from home before and aged just 21, Ruth was leaving behind her family, her friends, her life in Breslau and all that she was familiar with. There can be little doubt that she had no idea what lay ahead of her. Nor could she have known when or if she would ever see her family again.

Less than four months later, on 1 September 1939, Germany invaded Poland, an event that was to mark the beginning of the Second World War. Over the preceding six years, the world had stood idly by and watched as Hitler had gradually begun to exert more and more power over Germany and to put his plan of European domination into action. All attempts to reason and negotiate with him had ended in broken promises and failure. Nothing, it seemed, could break his resolve to once again make Germany a great, powerful and proud nation after having suffered the humiliation of defeat in the First World War.

The Second World War was to last for six years and, by the time that it was finally over at the beginning of September 1945, it is estimated to have cost more than 72 million lives. This was the first truly global war and was one of the worst conflicts in modern history in terms of its spread and sheer loss of life. It left no part of the world untouched. North America, South America, Europe, Asia, Africa and all the oceans in between were involved in one way or another.

The numbers of fatalities in some of the larger countries involved in the conflict are simply staggering: Soviet Union – 25 million, China – 15 million, Germany – 8 million and Poland – 5.5 million. Yet hidden deep within these stark numbers is one particular statistic that the world has since come to regard with a sense of utter shame and disbelief. A total of six million Jews were systematically murdered as part of Hitler's master plan to create a pure Aryan race and for Germany to once again become a dominant world power.

Land		Zahl
A. Altreich		131.800
Ostmark		43.700
Ostgebiete		420.000
Generalgouvernement		2.284.000
Bialystok		400.000
Protektorat Böhmen und Mähren		74.200
Estland – judenfrei –		
Lettland		3.500
Litauen		34.000
Belgien		43.000
Dänemark		5.600
Frankreich / Besetztes Gebiet		165.000
Unbesetztes Gebiet		700.000
Griechenland		69.600
Niederlande		160.800
Norwegen		1.300
B. Bulgarien		48.000
England		330.000
Finnland		2.300
Irland		4.000
Italien einschl. Sardinien		58.000
Albanien		200
Kroatien		40.000
Portugal		3.000
Rumänien einschl. Bessarabien		342.000
Schweden		8.000
Schweiz		18.000
Serbien		10.000
Slowakei		88.000
Spanien		6.000
Türkei (europ. Teil)		55.500
Ungarn		742.800
UdSSR		5.000.000
Ukraine	2.994.684	
Weißrußland ausschl. Bialystok	446.484	
Zusammen:	über	11.000.000

The Wannsee List

In preparation for the Wannsee conference which took place in Berlin on 20 January 1942, Adolf Eichmann had prepared a list showing the number of Jews living in Europe, classified by individual countries. The total number at the bottom of the list was 11 million. Although by 1945, he had been in power for just 13 years, Adolf Hitler had succeeded in wiping out more than half of the entire Jewish population of Europe.

It is impossible to hazard even a wild guess at how many millions of families in every corner of the globe were directly or indirectly affected by the industrial-scale slaughter of human life that took place during the Second World War. It would certainly not be overstated to say that there is hardly a single family today across much of the world that did not suffer some sort of loss, hardship, anguish or tragedy as a result of the collective madness that swept across Europe and the Asia-Pacific region between 1939 and 1945. And nowhere is this anguish felt more acutely than among Jewish families. To belong to a people whose members were systematically hunted down, persecuted, humiliated, tortured and murdered and to attempt to understand that more than half of your fellow Jews have been obliterated from the face of the earth is to test the strength of human endurance and belief in the goodness of humankind to its absolute limit. The full horror of the Holocaust lies beyond the powers of human comprehension.

Ruth Böhm was just one of millions of young Jewish women whose lives were changed forever as a result of the satanic vision of just one man. In many ways, her story is no different from that of countless other Jews who were forced to flee Germany and build a new life in a foreign land whose culture, language and traditions were completely alien to them. But Ruth Böhm was my mother, and this book is an attempt to piece together the story of her family, to trace its roots from its beginnings in rural Upper Silesia through the first two decades of the 20th century to the plebiscite of 1921. Our story will follow the economic chaos of the late 1920s, Hitler's rise to power in 1933 and the alienation, persecution and murder of the Jews that followed the momentous Wannsee resolution to embark on the 'Final Solution'. We will explore the utter destruction and sense of hopelessness of the war years and, in the years of peace following the Second World War, the survival, continuation and renewal of this now dispersed family in Australia, South America, Israel, the United States and the United Kingdom.

My personal fascination with this story began decades ago when I was a teenager growing up in South Wales. Although my mother avoided talking about Germany, the war and Hitler wherever possible, making a point of leaving the room if there were ever a TV programme being shown that dealt with this period in German history, she did at times like to share certain details about her early life in the 1920s. She described an idyllic childhood in Katscher, a small country town of around 8,000 people in Upper Silesia nestled among rolling meadows and lush farmland about a 30-minute drive from the much bigger town of Ratibor and around 100 miles south of Breslau, which was the capital city of the Prussian province of Silesia until 1945 when this part of Germany was handed over to Poland. She described how the family would often drive across the Czech border, which was situated very close to Katscher, to enjoy a day's shopping in Opava (Troppau). She told me how fond she was of her grandparents and that they lived in a stylish house on the outskirts of the town and that this was where all the major family gatherings took place. She painted a picture of a wealthy, middle-class family with a successful drapery business that was accustomed to living in large houses with maidservants, could afford expensive clothes and fine furniture and was clearly highly respected within the community.

However, she never really spoke very much about her life during the period between 1930 when Ruth and her family moved to Breslau and 1939 when she managed to get to the United Kingdom. The reason for this only became clear when I was in the middle of doing the research for this book. According to my eldest brother, Peter, whom Ruth had often confided in on such subjects, she had frequently said that her idyllic childhood had come to an abrupt end when she was aged just 12, in other words, in 1930. This was the year her parents uprooted the family and were forced to move to Breslau where they were to live in considerably more modest circumstances than those they had enjoyed in Katscher. It is clear that her early, formative years were spent living in a comfortable and secure environment in the countryside surrounded by a close, extended family and that this had all come to a sudden halt when her father, Arthur Böhm, was forced to sell the family business that he had taken over from his father, Louis, following his (Louis's) retirement.

My mother often intentionally excluded certain crucial details whenever she talked about her early life and could even be rather secretive. Perhaps she did this because there were certain episodes in her past which were just too painful for her to talk about, or maybe she did it simply to protect her children from knowledge that might adversely affect their lives. I have always felt a sense of sadness about this aspect of her character, and for years I greatly regretted not pushing her harder for more details about her childhood and teenage years because there was so much she told me that simply did not make sense. I could never fully understand why my mother and so many other members of her family had left Germany so abruptly in the 1930s to seek refuge in such far-flung corners of the world as Australia, Palestine, Peru and China. The reason of course that I could not make sense of this was that, once the war was over, my mother had clearly made a conscious decision never to tell her children that she was Jewish.

Like many other youngsters in the 1960s, I knew very little about the Holocaust and the horrific events that had taken place in Germany during the time that Hitler was in power. Nor do I remember ever learning about this period of German history during my time at grammar school in Pontypool. Had I known when I was a teenager the real reason so many Germans were forced to flee their country, I may well have put two and two together and naturally reached the conclusion that my mother had had to leave Germany because she was Jewish. But she chose not to tell us, and as a result, I do not think that it would be an exaggeration to say that we never really understood her. Sadly, the full extent of the trauma and hardship she had to endure in Germany in the 1930s and then during the war years in England was only revealed to us after her death in October 1977. My eldest brother, Peter, had always been very interested in European history and, after reading about the Holocaust some years earlier, he had guessed that our mother must be Jewish. When he confronted her with this assumption, she admitted that this was indeed the case but made him promise never to tell any of his brothers. However, shortly after our mother's funeral, Peter, called us all together and simply announced that Ruth was Jewish, which of course meant that we were also Jewish. This completely unexpected news was met with silence as we simply stood there, open-mouthed and in a state of shock.

But for my part, I have always been immensely proud of my German-Jewish heritage, as it is an integral part of who I am today. Although we do not always like to admit it, we are often shaped more by the past than by the present. There is an old Maori proverb that says, "We should always approach the future with our backs to it." I believe that I have been affected by the Holocaust in a way that others of my generation have not because I form part of an unbroken line that connects me directly to those members of my family who lived and, in some cases, died during the Holocaust. Persecution, alienation, fear, humiliation, violence, loss of identity and homeland are all woven into the very fabric of my family and can never be fully erased.

When I decided in 2017 that I wanted to attempt to write the story of the Böhm family, I was fully aware that this would not be an easy task. More than 80 years had passed since Hitler had come to power in 1933, so most of the members of the family who had lived through and survived the Holocaust had since died. Although I had access to a certain amount of information from the period in the form of letters, photographs, official documents and personal anecdotes, there can be no substitute for first-hand verbal accounts, and these were sadly lacking. I therefore decided that I would simply piece together those facts I could be sure of and then fill in any gaps in the account with, at best, an educated guess or, at worst, pure speculation based on my understanding of the story's main characters. So my main aim in attempting to write this book was to try to pull together all the various factual and anecdotal information that exists within the various branches of the Böhm family in Australia, the United Kingdom and the United States. However, it inevitably transpired that although I was able to discover a great deal of information about certain family members, I could find very little about some of the others. However, my principal objective throughout the writing process was to try to create a unified narrative rather than try to record every single event relating to each family member. My intention was to simply provide a general overview that follows the fortunes of the family during the early 1920s and 1930s in Katscher, Gleiwitz and Breslau through the war years and into the post-war period.

Although the starting point of the book focuses primarily on Louis and Jenni Böhm and their six children Arthur, Kate, George, Walter, Siegbert and Rudi (i.e. the first and second generations), I will also go into some considerable detail about the third generation of the family, in other words, Ilse, Ruth, Henry, Edith, Margot, Gary and Steffi (see family tree). There are two main reasons for devoting large segments of the book to this generation. Firstly, they all fled Germany at a very young age, generally in their late teens or early 20s, so their stories are therefore particularly poignant, and secondly, there was considerably more documentary material available for this generation than for the earlier generations.

Having embarked on this project, I quickly realized that if I were going to be able to actually complete the book, I would have to find a way to overcome one fairly significant obstacle. Many events covered in my account took place decades earlier, and as stated above, virtually all of the people who lived through the period covered by the book are now dead. Furthermore, the number of relevant first-hand documentary accounts, photographs and other materials still in existence was severely limited. This led me to realize that, inevitably, there would be significant gaps in my narrative and that I was therefore going to need to find a way to fill these gaps without allowing myself to drift off into the realms of fiction.

I decided to consult a journalist friend who was able to suggest how I could write a chronological narrative without any gaps and without detracting from the veracity of the overall account. His suggested solution was simply to refer to other peoples' contemporary accounts of the specific period and places in question and then to 'weave' this additional detail into the narrative of this book. As stated above, in 1930, my mother and her sister, Ilse, and their parents moved into an apartment in Breslau where they lived until shortly before the start of the war. However, we know almost nothing about their lives during this period. Fortunately, I was able to find a particularly detailed account (Willy Cohn: *No Justice in Germany – the Breslau Diaries 1933–1941*) that describes the everyday life of middle-class Jews living in Breslau during this same period. This made it possible for me to speculate with a fair degree of accuracy what my mother and her family might have experienced during these 'missing' years.

Clearly, speculation and truth are two distinct things, but I believe that if such speculation is based on factual contemporary information which is then set against what we actually know about the personality and behaviour of the various family members, then we can reasonably assume that our 'reconstructed' version of events may not be too far removed from the actual truth. In Part One of the book, my primary aim therefore was to create a cohesive and, wherever possible, factually correct account of the Böhm family covering the period from before the First World War until the late 1950s. I have tried to record all the events we know about chronologically to enable the story to flow better, and where necessary, I have indulged in some cautious speculation to fill in some of the inevitable gaps in my account.

The main focus of Part Two is to provide a brief overview of the region of Upper Silesia and to give an account of the terrible events that took place in Katscher, Gleiwitz and Breslau in 1945 as the war was ending. All these towns had at various times been home to the Böhm family before most of the family's members were forced to leave the country. This section of the book will conclude with an assessment of the dramatic transformation that Upper Silesia has undergone since becoming part of Poland in 1945. I believe that this is particularly relevant because this area was and remains the spiritual homeland of the Böhm family.

Part Three is devoted primarily to the trip I made with my daughter to Breslau, Katscher, Ratibor and Auschwitz in September 2018 as part of the research I carried out prior to starting to write the book. I will also give a brief account of my first-ever visit to Katscher in 1996. My daughter, Lucy, had always shown a keen interest in the background of her grandmother's family. We based ourselves in Breslau (today Wroclaw, Poland) and spent a couple of days exploring this fascinating city. Originally planned simply as an information-gathering venture, the week we spent in Upper Silesia subsequently evolved into an emotional and deeply meaningful journey back in time as we gradually retraced the footsteps of the Böhms. Sitting in the autumn sun at a restaurant on Breslau's fashionable 'Rynek' or standing in front of the apartment building where my great-uncle George and his wife, Elfriede, had once lived vividly brought the story of this exceptional family to life. In Katscher, we had the unique privilege of sitting in the very room where, over a period of 50 years, my great-grandparents Louis and Jenni had experienced so much and entertained so many members of their family. The day we spent inside the house on Thrömerstrasse was for both of us a truly humbling and uniquely moving experience.

Although Breslau was almost completely destroyed by the Soviets early in 1945 when their troops razed the city to the ground during its advance westwards towards Berlin, much of the city centre has now been restored to its former glory and looks very stylish and cosmopolitan, although many of the outlying suburbs still appear rather drab and run-down with a distinctly Soviet feel to them. Lucy and I were hoping to achieve several things during our week's stay in Poland. Firstly, we wanted to gain an impression of what daily life in the city might have been like during the 1930s. We also intended to visit the city's two railway stations. The main railway station is significant because it is from here that my mother and the other family members who managed to emigrate would have begun their journey to a new life in another country. But we also hoped to visit the Odertor station, the history of which is somewhat more sinister. For it was from here in the period 1941–1942 that more than 7,000 Jews, including my maternal grandmother Clara Böhm, were deported in cattle trucks to extermination camps in Poland, Germany and Czechoslovakia. Before leaving for Poland, we had already decided to visit the famous White Stork Synagogue in Breslau, which was the only synagogue in the city to survive the destruction of Kristallnacht in November 1938.

Also on our itinerary was a visit to Grüssau Monastery (today, Krzeszow, Poland) which the Germans commandeered in 1941 and converted into a transit camp for Jews being transported to Auschwitz (today, Oswiecim, Poland) and Theresienstadt (today, Terezin, Czech Republic). Clara Böhm was held in the monastery for about four months following her arrest in November 1941 before, we believe, she was sent to Theresienstadt. Then we hoped to travel south to Katscher (today, Kietrz, Poland), the town where Louis and Jenni Böhm, my great-grandparents, first set up home, created a thriving business and subsequently raised their six children. I knew from my previous visit in 1996 that the actual house in which Louis and Jenni had lived was still standing and was now occupied by a Polish family. Fortunately, with the help of the internet and social media, I had managed to make contact with this family, and over a period of about six months, we gradually began to exchange information about the house and its history and to build up a picture of what everyday life in the town might have been like for the Böhm family. Also on our agenda was a visit to the neighbouring town of Ratibor (today, Racibórz, Poland), which is much larger and is situated around eight miles from Katscher and would have featured significantly in the life of the Böhm family during the first two decades of the 20th century. The final stop on our agenda was a visit to the Auschwitz/Birkenau concentration camp, which is situated about 60 miles east of Katscher. I am happy to report that we managed to achieve everything that we had set out in our original plan, but before I relate all the details of our memorable trip to Upper Silesia, we must first go back to the year 1860, which is where the real story begins.

PART I

A FAMILY BORN TO SURVIVE

THE BEGINNINGS OF A DYNASTY

Jenni and Louis Böhm

My great-grandfather Louis Böhm was born in 1860 to Salomon Böhm and Charlotte Goldstab in Miechowitz, Beuthen (Bytom), Upper Silesia. Louis's parents were married in August 1852. Situated approximately 50 miles east of Ratibor, Beuthen was quite a large industrial town which in 1860 had a population of around 230,000 people. Since the Middle Ages, the surrounding area had been rich in natural resources, predominately iron, zinc and coal. As early as

1810, it had even boasted one of the largest privately owned ironworks in Germany, complete with its own coke blast furnace. Beuthen had always had strong Slavic influences, with a majority of people being Polish speakers. However, by 1910, following substantial population growth, approximately 60 per cent of the people living in the town were German speaking.

Louis had two brothers, Gustav and Salo, and two sisters, Jettel and Friederike. Although his father's profession is simply recorded as 'manager', it was not possible to determine whether he was involved in the drapery trade or some other profession. However, Jews had for centuries been attracted to the cloth trade, so I believe that in choosing the career path that he did, Louis may well have been following in his father's footsteps. Also, because we know that he set up his own business shortly after leaving home to get married, we can assume that he had received some previous training in this line of work, probably from his father. In February 1884, at the age of 24, Louis married Jenni Berger. As was customary at this time within the Jewish community, this would almost certainly have been an arranged marriage. But the two were obviously well matched and were to enjoy a long, happy marriage.

Jenni Berger was born in 1862 in the neighbouring town of Ratibor to Adolf Berger and Henriette Fröhlich. She came from a large family and had four sisters, Rosa, Regina, Ella and Olga, in addition to two brothers, Kurt and Simon. As far as I have been able to ascertain, Olga was the only sister never to marry.

While conducting my research for this book, I discovered that Louis had initially set up a small shop in Ratibor, probably sometime in the late 1800s, before opening a much bigger store in Katscher. Because Jenni came from Ratibor, it is possible that the young couple had initially set up home in the town and opened a shop there before moving to Katscher at a later date. We believe that the store in Katscher was quite large and, at its height, probably employed between eight and ten people.

Aerial View of Katscher c. 1930

The Böhm business seemed to have been mostly involved in the sale of men's and women's clothes, material and linen. A newspaper advertisement from this period confirms that Louis's shop was indeed originally situated in Ratibor and that he was interested in buying 'good-quality goose feathers' (pierze gesie). Because they were very soft and had no quills, goose feathers were frequently used in the down linings of jackets.

Newspaper advertisement

Interestingly, this advertisement was published in Polish, reflecting the fact that there was a large Polish population in this region, and it is almost certain that Louis spoke both German and Polish, as did most of the people who lived in this part of Silesia at that time. This advertisement would also support the theory that Louis may have been involved in some small-scale production. Even if he did not actually make any clothes himself, it has been well documented that there were many self-employed tailors living in Katscher, some of whom would have undoubtedly sub-contracted their services to local retail establishments.

Another reason Louis and Jenni decided to establish their business in Katscher was because of the town's long tradition of weaving and dyeing. These industries would have provided the Böhm's shop with a reliable local source of cloth and finished woven products. In a short memoir written just before she died, Ruth Böhm describes her grandfather's shop as 'the biggest ladies and gents outfitters in town', adding that the business was very successful and that the shop was always full of customers.

The Böhm's shop in Katscher

In addition to establishing their successful drapery business, Louis and Jenni were also clearly intent on starting a family as soon as possible, and over a period of 13 years, starting in 1885, Jenni gave birth to six children – five boys and a girl. While this may seem to have been a large family by today's standards, it was probably perfectly normal for the late 1800s. Many children died in childbirth in those days, so having a large number of children was considered the best way to ensure that couples could achieve the large families they desired.

Arthur was the oldest and was born in December 1885. George was born three years later in 1888, followed by Siegbert in 1889, Walter in 1893, Kate in 1895 and Rudi, the youngest, was born in November 1898. Although still factually unsubstantiated at the time of this writing, it is now believed that Rudi died as a young child around the age of seven, probably as a result of scarlet fever, which was prevalent during this period. The fact that he does not appear in one single family photograph and that there is no reference to him in any of the letters between the other brothers and Louis and Jenni would seem to strongly suggest that he must have died early in his life.

There exists a rumour within the family that has been passed down from generation to generation that Jenni was heartbroken by the loss of her youngest child and never fully got over it. I have recently commissioned a search for his death certificate, but until such time that any official document comes to light that proves conclusively that he died as a child, the only thing that we can say with any certainty is that he was born on 14 November 1898 in Katscher.

Although little is known about the children's early life in Katscher, we can assume that they were brought up according to strong Silesian and Jewish traditions and that theirs was a comfortable life within a stable family environment. Official records show that in 1910, there were only 52 Jews living in Katscher. The town had always been predominantly Catholic, so the Jewish population, though well integrated, had always represented a small minority and had never exceeded more than 200 people, even in the heyday of the early 1800s.

In Ruth's short account of her early life in Katscher, she remarks that, although the family was not overly religious, its members were expected to regularly attend the small synagogue that existed in the town. Louis certainly used to routinely go himself and apparently, on Yom Kippur, would always insist on drinking his customary cup of coffee before spending the day at the synagogue.

Early photographs suggest that Louis probably bought the 'villa' at No. 3 Thrömerstrasse in the late 1880s, shortly after getting married and setting up the family business. For its time, this was a very stylish house situated in one of the most fashionable streets on the outskirts of Katscher.

Market square Katscher 1920s

The house boasted an extremely large garden, complete with an elegant gazebo, and the interior had many high-quality wooden features, expensive furnishings and stylish cornices. We can, I think, assume that as they grew up, all five children were expected to help out both at home and in the family business while attending the local school in Katscher. The house was full to capacity at this time, as Jenni's ageing mother, Henriette Fröhlich, lived for many years in the attic room before her death in January 1916.

Home from the War 1918. Left to right: Walter, Kate, unknown, Siegbert, George, Louis, Jenni, Arthur

But the domestic situation was to change dramatically when all four boys were drafted into the army in 1914 and were sent to the front to fight in the Great War. So in 1915, Louis and Jenni hired Anna Jaschke as a housekeeper/cook. Her job was to run the household while Louis and Jenni managed the business.

Louis & Jenni's house in Thrömerstrasse c. 1935

Anna proved to be an extremely loyal employee and stayed with the family for more than 25 years. Miraculously, all four sons survived the war, and Arthur, who had been a medical orderly, was even awarded the German Iron Cross after being badly wounded at the Battle of Verdun in 1916 while rescuing a wounded soldier from the line of fire. He was struck in the face by shrapnel and sustained a serious injury which left his face badly disfigured for the rest of his life. His brother George was also awarded the Iron Cross for bravery.

Ruth recalls that sometime around 1928, Arthur had become ill with 'shock' as a result of his experiences during the First World War. What she was describing was undoubtedly some kind of PTSD, but she also says that he seemed to recover after an operation sometime later. He may well have undergone some kind of reconstructive surgery to improve the appearance of the left side of his face which had been badly disfigured as a result of his injuries.

As the oldest son, Arthur was also the first to marry, probably in 1911. Once again, this was an arranged marriage to Clara Heymann who would have been aged around 20, having been born in November 1891 in Rutenau, a town which, prior to 1935, was known by its Polish name of Chróścice. Following the end of the Second World War and the handing over of this part of Germany to Poland, Rutenau reverted to its former name.

Clara came from an extremely well-to-do, probably aristocratic, family. According to my mother, she was intelligent, cultured, very well-read and had a keen interest in all the arts, particularly music, and by all accounts was an accomplished pianist. She had one sister, Erna, and a brother, Friedrich. Tragically, following his marriage to Frida Wachsmann, both Friedrich and Frida would later die in Auschwitz.

The marriage between Arthur and Clara appears to have been something of a mismatch from the very outset, as anecdotal evidence and various references to her husband in Clara's later letters suggest that theirs was by no means a happy union. According to my mother, Arthur was apparently a very vain man who always seemed to have an eye for other women and would frequently put his own needs before those of his wife or family.

Clara Heymann

Ruth often told me that he liked to spend money on cars and stylish clothes and that she vividly remembers frequent outings across the border to Czechoslovakia where the car would be loaded up with cigarettes, fine food and other goods, which must have been significantly cheaper than in Germany at that time. By all accounts, Clara could often be rather fiery, and there were many arguments between her and Arthur, although it is not known what their disagreements were about or whether they were able to resolve them.

Ilse was born in April 1913, and five years later in February 1918, Ruth came along. One reason for the long gap between the births of the two daughters would undoubtedly have been the fact that Arthur was away fighting at the front although in all likelihood, he would have been invalided out of the army early as a result of his injury.

It may have been the case that, because of his horrific experiences at the front, Arthur had returned from the war a changed man like thousands of other veterans. We can imagine that, for someone so vain about his appearance, it must have been exceedingly difficult for him to come to terms with being disfigured so badly and, although this can in no way excuse his selfish behaviour, it may help explain why their marriage apparently continued to deteriorate after 1918.

In her last letters, Clara often speaks in very disparaging terms both about her husband and the Böhm family in general. As she had come from an upper-class background, I believe that she rather looked down on her in-laws, regarding them as nothing more than a family of shopkeepers. However, I think it is significant that the only person she seemed to really like and respect was George who, interestingly, was the only one to have received a university education and to take up a recognised profession (dentistry).

Ruth often told me that she was very happy growing up in Katscher and realised early on that she belonged to a wealthy family. In 1924, with the help of a substantial mortgage from the bank, Arthur bought one of the grandest villas in the town and subsequently employed two maids and a nanny who remained with the family for several years and whom my mother became extremely fond of. Although the house no longer exists, it was one of the largest houses in the town centre and had previously belonged to the former mayor of Katscher, Eugen Kodron who took up office in 1901. Census records from 1928 confirm that the house in Promenadenstrasse belonged to Arthur Böhm at that time and that for many years was always referred to locally as 'Villa Böhm' or 'Villa Kodron'.

'Villa Böhm'

I feel sure that Arthur would have been delighted and proud to own a house with such an impressive provenance. Following the end of the war, the house stood derelict for many years before being finally demolished in the early 1960s.

Ruth said that her parents were good to her but that she did not see much of them, as it would appear that the nanny was primarily responsible for bringing up the two girls. Ruth apparently enjoyed her schooldays but became unhappy when she was told that she would not be able to go to church like her other school friends. When she complained about this to her parents, they told her that she was Jewish and that she would have to undergo training in Jewish doctrines and start attending the synagogue.

Arthur was passionate about the outdoors and sport, particularly swimming and motor racing, and as she got older, Ruth quickly began to share his passion for the water. But she also used to enjoy just sitting on the floor of the drawing room listening to her mother singing and playing waltzes by Franz Lehar and Strauss.

In the short memoir she wrote about her early life, she says that Clara had a quick temper so, as has already been stated, there must certainly have been some conflict in the household. She absolutely adored her grandfather Louis and describes him as a 'peacemaker' who was never snobbish and always took the time to help anyone who needed his advice or guidance. She says that Louis was well respected in Katscher, was very popular and that people would always drop in to see him whenever they were passing.

Family photo c. 1926

Left to right, front row: Margot, Gary, Jenni, Steffi, Louis, Ruth, Henry. Back row: Clara, Elfriede, Friedrich Heymann (Clara's brother), George, Siegbert, Ilse, Edith, Arthur, Walter, Margarete

Apparently, Arthur, like his brother Siegbert, had originally trained as a tailor and although he continued to help his father in the family business after the war, he was ill-suited to the commercial world, as his big love seems to have been farming rather than retailing. His poor commercial grasp later had dire consequences for the thriving business Louis and Jenni had worked so hard to build.

In April 1912, Arthur's younger brother George married Elfriede Koslowsky, who was just 19 years old at the time and came from the neighbouring town of Bauerwitz (Leobschütz). Just 12 months later, she gave birth to their first child, Edith, in Gleiwitz where George was still training to be a dentist. Once again, because of the war, their second child Henry was not born until October 1920.

Elfriede Koslowsky

Unlike his brothers who had remained in Katscher, George and Elfriede had decided to set up home in Gleiwitz, a town situated approximately 55 km from Katscher.

With a population of more than 100,000 in the 1920s, Gleiwitz is a very old town, dating back to 1276, and was considerably larger and more cosmopolitan in character than Katscher was. It even boasted its own airport and although there was a great deal of industry there, Gleiwitz had a very stylish and fashionable city centre with many elegant streets and boulevards, swimming pools, a castle and extensive leisure facilities. It is not hard to see why George and Elfriede were keen to build a life for themselves in this vibrant, commercial centre rather than in a sleepy rural area such as Katscher.

In addition, George must have realised that this would be a much better place to set up a dental practice once he had finished his training. The family enjoyed a very comfortable life in Gleiwitz. They were well off financially, lived in a large house, took frequent skiing holidays in Switzerland and even had their own chauffeur.

George and Elfriede also had a large garden plot in the city where they spent many weekends growing their own vegetables.

Walter Böhm was five years younger than his brother George and, although it was not possible during my research to establish exactly when he married Margarete Berger, it would be reasonable to assume that the wedding took place sometime in the period 1920–1922 when he would have been around 27 years of age.

Their first daughter Gerda was born in 1924, but unfortunately she did not live beyond her sixth birthday and although the cause of her death is unknown, we can assume that she also died of one of several childhood illnesses which were prevalent at that time. No birth certificate could be found for Walter and Margarete's second daughter, Margot, but she was probably born sometime between 1926 and 1931.

Kate was two years younger than her brother Walter, and it is interesting that her husband to be, Henry Schweiger, was actually born in Beuthen, the same town Louis's family had come from. His parents were Fedor Schweiger and Sara Perls. Could it be that Käthe and Henry's marriage was also 'arranged', as it is more than likely that the two families knew each other? It is not clear when they got married, but their first child Gary was born in Tarnowitz, Upper Silesia, in 1921. Because it was often the case that newly married couples had their first child one or two years after marrying, we can assume that Henry and Kate were married sometime around 1919.

Tarnowitz, where the young couple set up home and started their own shoe-making business, was a fashionable town with around 86,000 inhabitants. Once again, it is not clear why they made the decision to leave Katscher and to move to a bigger and undoubtedly livelier town, but Louis may have helped them settle there because Tarnowitz was essentially a sub-district of Beuthen where Louis's family lived and where he himself had been born and brought up.

Kate and Henry Schweiger

Their second child, a daughter, Steffi, was born in 1924. In spite of what must have been a promising start to their married life, the young couple was about to experience a very tumultuous period early in their marriage as a result of a rapidly changing political climate and the considerable civil unrest that had broken out in this part of Silesia.

The Upper Silesia plebiscite was a referendum mandated by the Versailles Treaty and was conducted on 20 March 1921 to determine a section of the border between Weimar Germany and Poland. In fact, Henry was born just four days after the referendum had taken place. Under the previous rule by the German Empire, Poles claimed that they had been facing increasing levels of discrimination and were being made to feel like second-class citizens.

Plebiscite advertisement 1921

The period of the plebiscite campaign and inter-Allied occupation was marked by significant levels of violence across the entire region. In fact, three separate Polish uprisings occurred, and German volunteer paramilitary units were sent to the area in an attempt to restore order. For a time, the area was policed by French, British and Italian troops and overseen by an Inter-Allied Commission of Control. The Allies planned a partition of the region, but a Polish insurgency took control of over half of the area.

The Germans responded with volunteer paramilitary units from all over Germany to fight against the Polish units. In the end, following renewed Allied military intervention, the final position of the opposing forces became roughly where the new border would be located. The final decision was then handed over to the League of Nations, which confirmed the new border, and Poland received roughly one-third of the plebiscite zone by area, including the greater part of the industrial region.

Approximately 60 per cent of the population of Tarnowitz consisted of Poles, whereas Germans made up the remainder.

However, the result of the Plebiscite was that 61 per cent of people voted for the region to remain as part of Germany, whereas 38 per cent voted in favour of it becoming part of Poland.

The final decision to divide the region was made at an ambassador's conference in Paris. The German-Polish Accord on East Silesia (Geneva Convention), a minority treaty which dealt with the constitutional and legal future, was finally ratified on 15 May 1922.

Following the ratification of the treaty, life for many of the Germans living in the area quickly became increasingly difficult, as most of the Poles now wanted all Germans to leave the area immediately. It is not known when this hostility among the native Poles living in this area turned to violence, but sometime later, the Schweiger's shoe business was looted and burned to the ground and as the family was now effectively homeless, the only option was to return to Katscher and move in with Louis and Jenni.

We know, however that sometime towards the end of 1923 or early in 1924, they returned to Tarnowitz, perhaps believing that the situation had by then improved. They were apparently able to stay just long enough for Kate to give birth to her daughter Steffi who was born in 1924 before they were once again expelled from the town and had to return to Katscher.

THE GATHERING STORM

In 1925, Louis was 65 years old and had decided that the time was right for him to retire and pass the business on to another family member. It is not clear why he chose Arthur, but it may have been simply because he was the eldest son. By this time, George was already well established as a dentist in Gleiwitz and seemed to have shown no interest in managing the family shop. But I believe that it was with a degree of reluctance that Arthur finally took control of the business. His first love seemed to have been farming and the countryside, and by all accounts, he had never been particularly astute with money. This was undoubtedly one of the reasons the business declined rapidly between 1925 and 1930. However, Arthur's poor business sense was not the only reason the Böhm's store ultimately failed, as a very damaging global financial crisis was also looming.

The Great Depression was a global economic slump that erupted in the autumn of 1929 and then lasted for 10 years. It began just as an American crisis, specifically a huge stock market crash, but one which was to have knock-on effects around the world. The Great Depression was severely felt in Germany where it caused widespread unemployment, starvation and misery.

This period of hardship ultimately contributed to the rise of Adolf Hitler and the National Socialists (NSDAP). The effect on Weimar Germany was particularly dire. Germans were not so much reliant on exports as they were on American loans, which had been propping up the Weimar economy since 1924. From the autumn of 1929, no further loans were issued while American financiers began to call in all existing loans. Despite its rapid growth, the German economy could not endure this sudden retraction of cash and capital, and banks struggled to provide money and credit. In 1931, hyperinflation led to runs on both German and Austrian banks, resulting in many of them going out of business. Brüning's deflation policy of the early 1930s only seems to have made the situation worse.

In 1930, the United States, which by then was the largest purchaser of German industrial exports, put up tariff barriers to protect its own companies. German industrialists lost access to US markets and found credit almost impossible to obtain. Many industrial companies were forced to close factories completely or shrink dramatically. By 1932, German industrial production was at 58 per cent of its 1928 levels. One consequence of this decline was spiralling unemployment, but the effects on German society as a whole were truly devastating.

By the end of 1929, around 1.5 million Germans were out of work, and within a year, this figure had more than doubled. By early 1933, unemployment in Germany had reached six million, more than one-third of its entire working population. Although there were few shortages of food, millions found themselves without the means to obtain it. Children suffered worst, with thousands dying from malnutrition and hunger-related diseases. Millions of industrial workers, who during the 'Golden Weimar Age' had become the best-paid blue-collar workers in Europe, were to be unemployed for more than a year.

So sometime in 1930, the Böhm business in Katscher either went bankrupt or was sold, no doubt at a knockdown price. It was subsequently acquired by Max Cohn, a Jewish businessman who was also a friend of the family. An early photograph of Katscher would seem to confirm that, prior to taking over Louis's shop, Max Cohn had actually been managing a smaller business in the market square. As far as we know, the Cohn business continued to operate throughout the 1930s, but in 1942, Max Cohn was arrested and deported to Auschwitz where he died. Arthur and Clara were forced by the bank to sell their large villa in Katscher and decided to move to Breslau, some 160 kilometres to the north.

Breslau was one of Germany's largest cities at the time with a population of 625,000 people in 1930, of which 20,000 were Jewish. It is not clear why they chose Breslau, as there were a number of other large towns nearby, including Gleiwitz and Oppeln. Perhaps Arthur believed that his employment prospects would be better in such a large city. Together with their two daughters, Arthur and Clara moved into an apartment at No 11, Kronprinzenstrasse, which was one of the more fashionable streets in Breslau. Although it is not exactly clear how the family managed financially during this period, a 1935 census records Arthur's occupation being listed as 'Sales Representative', which would appear to make sense, as selling was probably one of the few skills he possessed at that time.

Kronprinzenstrasse Breslau

In 1935, Hitler introduced a number of new race laws as part of the Nazi's increasing determination to completely ostracise Jews. Mixed marriages would no longer be allowed, no Aryan maids over the age of 45 were to be employed by Jewish families, and from that time on, Jews were to be regarded as mere subjects of the state. In addition, many of the Jewish-owned restaurants in Breslau either went into liquidation or were forcibly closed on the purported grounds of 'uncleanliness', and many elderly Jews who had been arrested for 'moral violations' took their own lives rather than face the consequences.

Louis and Jenni's Golden Wedding Celebration 24 March 1934

Front row (left to right): Ella Wolf (Berger), Regina Weissenberg (Berger), Henry Böhm, Jenni Böhm, Louis Böhm, Rosa Rosenthal (Berger), Margarete Böhm, Gary Schweiger
Second row (left to right): Kate Schweiger, Siegbert Böhm, Steffi Schweiger, Ruth Böhm, Edith Böhm, Margot Böhm, Henry Schweiger, Arthur Böhm, Clara Böhm (Heymann)
Third row (left to right): Anna Jaschke, Elfriede Böhm, Olga Berger, Ilse Böhm, Kurt Berger, Salo Rosenthal
Fourth row (left to right): George Böhm, Simon Berger
Back row (left to right): Eric Wolf, Max Lustig, Walter Böhm

On 24 March 1934, the whole Böhm family assembled in the sitting room of the Thrömerstrasse villa to celebrate Louis and Jenni's golden wedding anniversary and even posed for a commemorative photo in front of the gazebo in the garden (see above). This would be the last occasion the whole family would gather together.

Hitler had already been in power for a year, and many Jews throughout Germany were beginning to realise that life was going to become increasingly difficult for them. However, under the guarantee that had formed part of the League of Nations treaty, Jews in most parts of Upper Silesia, an area encompassing around 1.5 million people and 10,000 Jews in 1933, had been granted special minority protection that barred Nazi discrimination on the basis of religion.

It is fair to say therefore that the limits on antisemitism enforced by the League of Nations in this eastern corner of the Reich amounted to something of an accident of history and was actually a consequence of a Polish-German treaty signed after the First World War. However, as a result of this anomaly, life for Jews living in Upper Silesia following the rise of Hitler was much more protected and comfortable than it was for Jewish people living in other parts of Germany.

This situation would remain largely unchanged until the dramatic turning point marked by Kristallnacht in November 1938. The wedding anniversary would undoubtedly have been a happy occasion for everyone present, but particularly for Louis and Jenni who loved nothing more than entertaining the whole family in their home.

There are a couple of very interesting observations that can be made from the above photograph. We know that Ilse Böhm was the first member of the family to leave Germany, and although we cannot be sure of exactly when she moved away from Katscher, anecdotal information within the family seems to suggest that she had actually left before Hitler came to power in 1933.

Ilse may have been more religious than other members of the family and, from an early age, had been very interested in and inspired by the Zionist movement. This movement was formed in Cologne in 1897 by Max Bodenheimer and by 1914 had attracted more than 10,000 members. In 1933, after Hitler had taken power, the so-called Haavara Agreement was drawn up between German Zionists and the Nazi regime to enable and encourage young German Jews to immigrate to Palestine.

Sometime in the early 1930s, Ilse joined the Zionist movement and went to Czechoslovakia as part of her training in Zionist doctrines. We can therefore assume that, as she is present in the above photograph, she must have returned briefly to celebrate her grandparent's golden wedding anniversary. She had already met Ze'ef Yoffe, Gidon's father, probably in Czechoslovakia, and immigrated to Palestine with him sometime later in 1934, most likely on a visa granted under the Haavara Agreement. Ilse's first son, Gidon, was born in Palestine in 1935, and just two years later, their second child, Tamar, a girl, was born. Ze'ef Yoffe later achieved considerable fame as a renowned Israeli cartoonist.

Only two people in the above photograph were not members of the extended family – Anna Jaschke was Louis and Jenni Böhm's housekeeper and cook who worked for the family for more than 25 years. Max Lustig was a family friend who came from Gleiwitz. In her book *Walter's Welcome*, Eva Neisser Echenberg tells the story of her uncle, Walter Neisser, a wealthy, influential Jew who originally came from Beuthen where Louis was born and brought up. Walter Neisser left Germany for Peru in the 1920s and, years later following Hitler's rise to power, helped many members of his own family and dozens of Jewish businessmen immigrate to Peru, often sponsoring them and employing them in his engineering factory. Walter Neisser's business partner in Lima was Rudolph Lustig, who was I believe Max Lustig's brother. It is therefore highly likely that Walter Neisser and Rudolph Lustig also helped Walter and Margarete Böhm along with their daughter Margot immigrate to Peru in October 1941.

One interesting footnote regarding Walter is that, on 13 February 1937, the Gestapo arrested and held him for just over a month in the Dachau concentration camp before releasing him. The only reason stated in the documentation is 'Jewish prisoner', and his arrest warrant simply states that he was transported to Dachau by train. It is notable that at no time after the war did Walter ever appear to show any interest in joining the rest of the family in Australia.

This leads me to conclude that Walter, Margarete and Margot must have been very happy in Lima. In fact, all three of them subsequently took up Peruvian citizenship. We also know that Margot married Max Anschlawski who also held Peruvian citizenship. We have very little information about him except that he was born in 1904, visited New York in July 1959 and, from 1996 onwards, seems to have been living in Miami, Florida. It is possible that he settled there following Margot's death in 1992. Margot's father, Walter, died in 1960. Both he and his daughter were buried in the Jewish cemetery in Lima.

Left to right: Ruth, Elfriede, Steffi, Henry, Kate and Henry c. 1935

As has already been mentioned in the prologue, information about everyday life within the Böhm family during the 1930s is rather limited, but we can make some assumptions based on what we do know and the political backdrop in Germany during this period.

Although Louis was no doubt enjoying his retirement in Katscher and George was practicing as a dentist in Gleiwitz, Arthur, Clara and Ruth were simply trying to survive as best they could in Breslau. By 1935, Ilse had already left for Palestine. As has already been stated, life for the Jewish population in Upper Silesia prior to Kristallnacht was far easier than it was for Jews living in other parts of Germany as a consequence of the League of Nations ruling. Kate and Henry had established another shoe business in Ratibor, whereas Siegbert, who as a homosexual was regarded as something of the black sheep of the family, had settled in Berlin sometime after 1935, where it is believed he had a boyfriend. However, a business directory from 1935 lists him as still living and working as a tailor in Waldenburg (Silesia). Not much is known about Walter and Margarete during this period or what line of business Walter was in, but we do know that in 1936, he and his wife were living in an apartment at Viktoriastrasse 47 in Breslau. Interestingly, both George and Elfriede and, I believe, Arthur and Clara also spent short periods living on this same street in the late 1930s.

ESCAPE AND INTERNMENT

Kindertransport statue in Berlin

There can be little doubt that the terrible events of Kristallnacht in November 1938 changed everything for the Böhms, as it did for tens of thousands of other Jewish families throughout Germany. Suddenly, the stark reality of what lay ahead for those Jews who had chosen to remain in Germany became clear, so the absolute priority for many was simply to get out of the country as soon as possible. For obvious reasons, there was a clear focus and urgency on getting the children and young people out of Germany first, and a number of international campaigns were established to assist in this critical task. The most successful and perhaps best-known of these initiatives was the Kindertransport campaign, which was also called the Refugee Children's Movement. Between the end of November 1938 and 1 September 1939, more than 10,000 children who, according to the Nuremberg Race Laws, were classified as Jewish, were sent from Germany and the other occupied countries to be resettled in Great Britain.

Following Kristallnacht, the British Parliament had responded to calls for action by the British Jewish Refugee Committee and held a debate in the House of Commons on 21 November 1938. Although the government had just imposed a new cap on Jewish immigration to Palestine as part of its mandate there, several factors contributed to its decision to permit an unspecified number of children under the age of 17 to enter the United Kingdom. These included the diligence of refugee advocacy, the growing awareness of anti-Jewish atrocities in Germany and Austria and pro-Jewish sympathies among some high-placed Britons. To "assure their ultimate resettlement", a £50 bond had to be posted for each of the children, who, it was assumed, would be reunited with their parents once the crisis had passed. They were issued temporary travel documents to enable their entry to Great Britain.

On 1 December 1938, less than one month after Kristallnacht, the first transport left Germany. It arrived in Harwich the following day, bringing 196 children from a Jewish orphanage in Berlin that had been burned to the ground by the Nazis on 9 November. Most of the subsequent transports left by train from Vienna, Berlin, Prague and other major cities (children from smaller towns travelled to meet the transports). The transports then crossed the Dutch and Belgian borders and from there continued on to England by ship. The majority of the children never saw their parents again.

The second member of the Böhm family to leave Germany was Ilse's sister Ruth. To ensure that she could get out as soon as possible, Clara and Arthur enlisted the help of the Anglo-German Agency, an organisation based in London engaged in helping young German women obtain suitable domestic service positions in Great Britain. This organisation was set up in 1931 by Lisbeth Röntgen Thomson, a German-born woman, and up until 1936, it was allowed to carry on its activities quite freely with the approval of the German authorities. On 31 March 1939, Ruth received a firm offer of a suitable post that had been identified for her in Great Britain. The job offer reads as follows:

'...a nice family living in a house in the country, close to Kings Langley, situated 21 miles from London. The household consists of four people (three ladies, one gentleman and a young girl). You will be expected to carry out all household duties, including 'middle-class' cooking. You will need to wear an apron at all times. Your salary will be £40 per year, i.e. 66 English shillings per month. There is a thirteen-year old daughter in the house. The house has 8 rooms and the ladies usually cook for themselves. No German will be spoken. This is a Protestant family which will provide you with a good home.'

Ruth promptly accepted the offer, and on 21 May 1939, aged just 21, she left Germany for good. She always maintained that the Sadler family was very kind to her and that it did indeed provide her with a good home. This part of Hertfordshire is quiet and delightfully rural even today. The village atmosphere of the town and its close-knit community would not have been too dissimilar from the environment where Ruth had grown up, so it is clear why she felt so much at home there.

The former Sadler home in Abbots Langley

I always remember that my mother was a very good cook, but I can imagine that, at this early stage of her life and never having lived away from home, her general housekeeping and cooking skills were probably quite limited. This would seem to be borne out by the fact that a year earlier, in March 1938, no doubt at the behest of her mother, Ruth had successfully completed a general housekeeping course at the Paula Ollendorff-Haushaltungsschule in Breslau.

In the correspondence between Ruth and her mother, Clara, during the summer of 1939, it is clear that Ruth was very happy with her new life in England and was even feeling optimistic about the future, although she was clearly missing her mother. In a very significant letter written by Clara to Ruth on 18 July 1939 while she was staying with George and Elfriede in Gleiwitz, it is made patently clear that all the necessary arrangements had been made for Clara to join her daughter in England.

'I am going to have to really hurry if I am supposed to be there on 1 September. I just can't quite believe it and I am going to have to get used to the idea. Drop me a line and let me know what you need and what I

should bring with me. I have received a long letter from Aunt Erna. She is really looking forward to it too. I just won't believe it until I am actually sitting on the ship.'

However, due to an absolutely tragic twist of fate, Clara would never leave Germany for, on the very day she was supposed to arrive in England, 1 September 1939, Germany invaded Poland and, two days later, Britain and France declared war on Germany. Clara and her daughter Ruth never saw each other again and, less than three years later, in May 1942, Clara died in Theresienstadt.

Ruth often talked to me about how the mood of the British public and its attitude towards the many Germans in its midst changed dramatically once war had been declared on Germany. There is one particular incident she could clearly never forget. Like her father, she had always been a keen swimmer and used to enjoy spending hours at the local swimming pool in her time off from her domestic service job. On one occasion in what must have been late summer of 1939, she was not only verbally abused by other people at the pool, but stones were actually thrown at her. As a naïve and sensitive young woman who had led a very sheltered life, this traumatic event must have affected her deeply. But she would soon have to endure much worse treatment at the hands of the very same people who had ostensibly offered her refuge from the harsh treatment she would have received back in Germany at the hands of the Nazis. Just three months later, at the beginning of December, Ruth resigned from her job with the Sadler family. In a letter of reference, her employer Florence Sadler writes:

'Ruth is leaving us to take up nursing. We have found her of good character, well-trained, keen and intelligent, wonderfully cheerful, good-tempered and anxious to please and improve herself in all ways.'

Fritz Pelikan's fellow inmates Kitchener Camp 1939

Fritz Pelikan

To my knowledge, my mother had never shown any interest in nursing, so we can therefore assume that there must have been some other reason for her to leave her job in Hertfordshire and travel down to Kent shortly before Christmas of that year. Back home in Germany, Ruth had become very close to Fritz Pelikan, who was born in Georgenberg, near Kattowitz and whose parents were good friends with Clara Böhm. Fritz, who seemed to be Ruth's unofficial boyfriend at the time, was released from Dachau in July 1939, having been granted an entry visa to the United Kingdom. By Christmas of that year, he had already been an inmate of the Kitchener camp in Richborough, Kent, for five months and then joined the Auxiliary Military Pioneer Corps, no doubt to secure his permanent residence in the United Kingdom.

Between February 1939 and the outbreak of the Second World War on 3 September 1939, almost 4,000 adult male Jewish refugees were put on trains from Berlin and Vienna. They travelled via Oostende and Dover to Sandwich in East Kent, where the CBF (Central British Fund for German Jewry) had rented an old First World War base known as the Kitchener camp.

This camp was one of seven WWI camps close to Sandwich, known collectively as Richborough Port. The camp itself was sometimes referred to, particularly by the Jewish philanthropists who ran the CBF, as 'Richborough Transit Camp'.

Two Jewish brothers, Jonas and Phineas May, ran the camp. They had both gained previous experience of running summer camps for the Jewish Lads' Brigade, but it would have been a much more demanding task to run a camp for 4,000 traumatized men, most of whom had been forced to leave behind their families in the Third Reich and in those countries now occupied by the Germans.

During the summer of 1939, a few of the men managed to get their families out of German-occupied territory by making use of the system of 'domestic service visas' for their wives and the Kindertransport for their children. However, most families were unable to escape Germany in time and were murdered during the Holocaust.

The Auxiliary Military Pioneer Corps, the unit Fritz Pelikan joined, was a British Army non-combat corps engaged in light engineering tasks. It was formed in 1939 and amalgamated into the Royal Logistic Corps in 1993. Pioneer units performed a wide variety of tasks in all theatres of war, including stretcher-bearing, handling all types of stores, laying prefabricated track on beaches and carrying out various logistical operations. Ruth may well have travelled down to the south coast to be with Fritz, although it is not entirely clear where she stayed or where she worked during this period. However, it is possible that she could have been helped by a lady called Joyce Piercy and her sister, Pat, who knew Ruth's family (and Fritz Pelikan) quite well. The Piercy sisters, who were well-known, lived close to the camp and often befriended young male Jewish inmates, inviting them to tea and taking them on trips around the local area. In his book *From Dachau to Dunkirk*, Fritz Pelikan recalls that he spent Christmas 1939 with the Piercy sisters, so it is entirely possible that Ruth was there as well.

We know, however, that by this time, there were already at least two other men in Ruth's life. Emil Brand was from Vienna and was also an inmate at the Kitchener camp at around the same time while he was waiting for his immigration visa to the United States to be approved. In Part Three, we will return to the subject of Emil Brand and how he and Ruth actually met, but we know for certain that they did get together, albeit briefly, either at the end of 1939 or very early in 1940. After her death in 1977, Ruth left behind a number of photographs, not only of members of her family but also of people who had obviously been very special to her. These include a number of both signed and unsigned photos of a young man called Rudi who we know was in Berlin in October 1938.

Ruth received a letter from her old friend Paul Wiener in July 1939 where it is made clear that Rudi was actually in England with Ruth during the months leading up to the outbreak of the Second World War.

'You have landed on your feet with your acquaintances there. So you have the most important things you need when you are in another country: support, help and advice. Make sure you keep these acquaintances. And you also have your Rudi there with you.'

Rudi

We cannot be sure whether Rudi was just a very good friend or whether their relationship was of a more intimate nature. But the fact that Ruth had kept so many different photos of him leads me to believe that theirs was probably a romantic attachment. As we have no surname for Rudi, it has not been possible to ascertain what happened to him after he arrived in England. However, in the first few months of 1940, Emil Brand sailed to the United States, and Fritz Pelikan, who was now an official member of the British Army, left for France.

Although life could not have been easy for the thousands of Germans and Italians who had already been living in the United Kingdom before the war broke out, they were allowed to continue with their everyday lives with a reasonable degree of freedom. This would though all change once the war got underway. In May 1940, Winston Churchill was elected prime minister, and later that same month, the dramatic and unprecedented Dunkirk evacuations began and continued until 4 June. Dunkirk was to significantly change the course of the Second World War, but its effect on the thousands of so-called enemy aliens living in the United Kingdom at the time was to prove to be even more dramatic.

In September 1939, around 80,000 potential enemy aliens were in

Britain, and following the start of the war, all Germans and Austrians over the age of 16 were ordered to appear before special tribunals to be classified into one of three groups:

- 'A' – those deemed to pose a high security risk, numbering just under 600, who were to be immediately interned;
- 'B' – 'doubtful cases', numbering around 6,500, who would be supervised and would be subject to restrictions;
- 'C' – 'no security risk', numbering around 64,000, who were left at liberty. More than 55,000 of category 'C' were recognised as refugees from Nazi oppression. The vast majority of these were Jewish.

Ruth appeared before her first tribunal on 13 October 1939 and was classified as a 'Category C enemy alien'. However, the situation began to change rapidly in the spring of 1940 when the failure of the Norwegian campaign led to an outbreak of spy fever and rising agitation against enemy aliens. More and more Germans and Austrians were rounded up, and Italians were also included, even though Britain would not be at war with Italy until June of that year. By that time, there were at least 19,000 Italians in Britain, and Churchill ordered them all to be arrested, despite the fact that most of them had lived in Britain for decades. The fact that many of the enemy aliens were Jewish refugees and were therefore hardly likely to be sympathetic towards the Nazis was a complication no one bothered to try to resolve. They were still treated as German and Austrian nationals. It is estimated that, in one Isle of Man camp alone, more than 80 per cent of the internees were Jewish refugees.

It is not clear how long Ruth remained on the south coast once Fritz Pelikan had left for France, but as a young single woman with virtually no knowledge of English, no job and no money, her options would have been severely limited. To complicate matters, she had now discovered that she was pregnant. So sometime in the early spring of 1940, she went to live with her Aunt Erna (Clara Böhm's sister) who was living in north London. I believe that, around 10–12 June, two policemen knocked on the door of 91, Dartmouth Road and arrested her. She was ordered to pack a small suitcase and to bring only the bare essentials with her. This must have been a deeply traumatizing experience for Ruth. In Breslau under the Nazi regime, everyone had lived in constant fear of the knock on the door and the awful consequences that could follow. But in coming to Great Britain, quite understandably, she believed that this was something that she would no longer have to be afraid of and that she would be protected and allowed to live in relative freedom and peace. My mother had always claimed that she had been arrested because someone had 'denounced' her. She would later share her suspicions with Emil Brand whom she was in contact with for at least a couple of years following her internment. But in a letter written to Ruth in May 1942, Emil tries to dismiss her suspicions.

'I think that you should stay in contact with Joyce because it is better to have one too many friends than one too many enemies. I cannot believe that she betrayed you and I think that you are just imagining this. Write to her because you might need her one day.'

I believe that the 'Joyce' referred to in Emil's letter was probably none other than Joyce Piercy who had befriended both Fritz Pelikan and Emil Brand during their time in the Kitchener camp. Before the war, Joyce and her sister, Pat, had always been very sympathetic towards the Jewish refugees, particularly the men. However, once the mass roundups had started in earnest and the authorities were faced with the huge task of identifying the whereabouts of tens of thousands of enemy aliens spread all over the country, could it be that Joyce Piercy had felt that it was her patriotic duty to 'report' Ruth if she knew where she was at this time? We will never know for sure, but my personal opinion is that I find it unlikely that Joyce Piercy would have betrayed the whereabouts of my mother given that she and her sister had gone to such great lengths to make life for those Jewish refugees arriving in Britain in 1939 more comfortable and enjoyable.

There can be little doubt that the British authorities were ill-prepared to implement Churchill's draconian plan to round up and imprison every enemy alien in the United Kingdom. Following her arrest, Ruth appeared before a second tribunal on 13 June 1940 at a magistrate's court in Hatfield, which is situated just 20 miles north of where she was living at the time. This time, the official court decision was that she was to be interned until further notice. However, having carried out the arrests and ordered the internments, the British authorities had no idea what to do with these thousands of people or where to put them. So as a temporary measure, they decided to do the only thing they could, which was to put them in prison. Immediately following her court appearance, Ruth was locked up in Holloway prison, which is an ugly, antiquated building that was originally opened in 1856 as a mixed prison. In 1903 though it became a female-only facility and remained as such until it was finally closed in 2016. By all accounts, conditions were extremely harsh, and I can only begin to imagine how terrified and abandoned my mother must have felt during the five weeks she spent there. Finally, on 18 July 1940, Ruth was sent to the Rushen internment camp on the Isle of Man.

Having being put on a train to Liverpool, she then boarded a cargo ship bound for Douglas, the main port on the Isle of Man. Authorities on the island had been asked by the British government to accommodate thousands of enemy aliens in the towns of Douglas, Ramsey and Peel. The majority of these people, like my mother, were refugees from Germany, but even German nationals who had lived in the United Kingdom for many years were also arrested and interned. The authorities on the Isle of Man decided that the only way so many people could be accommodated on such a small island was to simply commandeer all the hotels and guest houses.

Rushen Camp was unique in Europe, being the only women-only camp run entirely by women and, at its height, accommodated 3,500 inmates. Unlike the other camps on the island, Rushen camp was administered by the Home Office and not by the military, so conditions were far less harsh. However, the camp's notorious commandant, Dame Joanna Cruikshank, was heavily criticized for, among other things, not ensuring that genuine refugees were housed separately from the many Nazi sympathisers, and as a result, she was eventually removed from her post. Initially, Ruth was forced to share a room with a Jew-hater with strong Nazi sympathies. Her son, Peter, was born on 11 November 1940 in Waverley House, Rushen Camp.

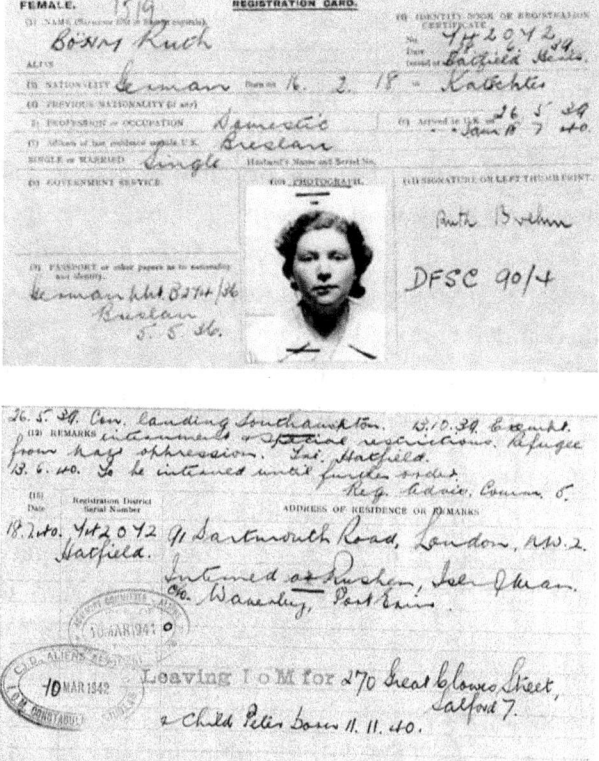

Ruth Böhm's Internment Order

To begin with, the women enjoyed a high degree of freedom and were even allowed to explore the pretty town of Port Erin. Their movements though were eventually curtailed, and barbed wire fences were erected around the camp, although they were still allowed limited access to the beach (the summer of 1940 was very hot). The women quickly organised themselves into groups and shared their skills to make a wide variety of activities available to everyone. These included cooking, sewing, sculpture, typing, dressmaking and music. Some beautiful work was produced and can still be seen today in the Rushen museum.

Some months after the camps had been established and things were running smoothly, the authorities set up a series of regular tribunals to assess the level of allegiance and risk the internees posed with a view to returning those people deemed to be low-risk to the mainland. As a result, many of the internees were allowed to leave after just six or nine months on the island, particularly if they had relatives or friends who could vouch for them or support them financially. Unfortunately, Ruth was not so lucky. I believe that she appeared before a tribunal on a number of occasions, and each time her application to leave was rejected.

Rushen Internment Camp

As a young, unmarried woman with a child, no resources, no job and no permanent address in Great Britain, she may have been deemed to have been too high-risk. Consequently, she was to remain in Rushen Camp until March 1942 when she was finally released.

An outcry in Parliament had led to the first releases of internees in August 1940. By February 1941, more than 10,000 had been freed, and by the following summer, only 5,000 remained in internment camps. Many of those released from internment subsequently contributed to the war effort on the home front or served in the armed forces. Ruth made many friends during her internment on the Isle of Man and, following her release, even managed to stay in contact with one young woman she had become particularly close to. Grete Weiner was a Jewish internee from Vienna who had been interned in May 1940. By a strange coincidence, she and Ruth had become pregnant at around the same time, but it was probably no coincidence that they both decided to name their baby sons Peter John. They no doubt believed that by choosing the most Christian names possible, these little Jewish boys would never have to experience the persecution and suffering their mothers had endured. We shall take up Ruth's story again when we begin to look at the post-war period. Now it is time to track the fortunes of those other members of the Böhm family who were also fortunate enough to escape the gathering storm in Nazi Germany.

Having been forced to leave their home in Tarnowitz in 1924 because of vehement anti-German feeling following the plebiscite that led to the complete destruction of their shop, Henry and Kate Schweiger moved in with Louis and Jenni in Katscher and subsequently set up another shoe business in nearby Ratibor. But sometime around 1935, when their business was again boycotted, Henry, Kate and the children moved north to Breslau, which at that time had one of the largest Jewish populations in the whole of Germany and where, they believed, there might at least be 'safety in numbers'. However, everything changed for thousands of Jews after Kristallnacht on 9 November 1938 when SA paramilitary forces carried out pogroms against Jews all over Germany. Jewish homes, hospitals and schools were ransacked as the attackers literally demolished whole buildings with sledgehammers. The rioters also destroyed 267 synagogues throughout Germany, Austria and the Sudetenland.

Gary Schweiger 1938

The Schweigers must have seen which way the wind was blowing because they had already applied for emigration some time before Kristallnacht. This would undoubtedly have been a long process, and of course there was no guarantee that a visa would be granted, because many countries were already closing their doors to the thousands of refugees desperate to get out of Germany. However, Henry and Kate were fortunate and, sometime in early November 1938, they boarded a ship in Hamburg bound for Genoa, Italy, where they then embarked on the S.S. Romolo, an Italian cargo ship heading for Freemantle in Australia. Interestingly, the entry in the ship's manifest shows that only their daughter, Steffi, travelled with them. Just two years later, in September 1940, Henry's father, Fedor, died in Gleiwitz.

Their son, Gary, continued living with his grandparents in Katscher for a while before leaving to join a Jewish youth camp in Czechoslovakia, where he actually got stuck for almost a year because of the worsening political climate and stricter border controls. In 1939, just before the borders were closed completely, Gary was lucky enough to escape and get to Holland where he boarded the P&O ship S.S. Narkunda bound for Australia via Liverpool and Marseille. Gary finally arrived in Freemantle in December 1939. Interestingly, this ship was subsequently converted into an auxiliary transport vessel but was torpedoed and sunk off the coast of North Africa in 1942.

Once they had arrived in Sydney, the first place Henry, Kate and Steffi lived was in the Kings Cross area where Kate was employed as a family cook. Later, they managed to set up a shoe repair business in Maroubra Bay, one of Sydney's eastern suburbs, but this was an extremely difficult time for the family. Kate literally had to tramp around on foot drumming up business within the large immigrant community. Having no means of transport, she would simply walk to her customers, collect the shoes, take them back to her shop to be repaired and then walk back to the customer to return the repaired shoes.

Sometime in 1941, their daughter, Steffi, met her future husband, Walter Friedlander (Freeman), who had also started working in the shop. By this time, Kate's son, Gary, had joined the family in Sydney and was now employed as an apprentice plumber. Walter and Steffi were married in 1944.

Walter Freeman and Steffi Schweiger

Anyone who managed to get out of Germany and gain entry to another country between the outbreak of the war in September 1939 and 1942, when the mass extermination of the Jews began in earnest, was undoubtedly extremely lucky. Yet the story of Henry Böhm's escape is surely nothing short of miraculous. As the dark clouds of war gathered in the late 1930s, many thousands of Germans who had suddenly become refugees, either because they were Jewish or because they were politically opposed to the Nazis, fled to Britain for sanctuary.

Henry Böhm

Few of them could have known that they would soon be deported to Australia in one of the more notorious incidents in British maritime history, later described by Winston Churchill as 'a deplorable mistake'. In 1938, Henry was living in Berlin with his Uncle Siegbert and was training to be a locksmith at an ORT school (ORT – Organisation, Reconstruction and Training – was a global Jewish education network with a network of schools in various countries). Years later, he recalled that, on one particular day in June 1940, the whole class was told to collect its belongings and report to a specific location where they were to be evacuated to England aboard a Kindertransport. On his arrival in Great Britain, Henry was interned for some months in Leeds where he was told that he had to wait for a 'hired military transport ship' that would take him to Australia.

As a wave of fear about an imminent German invasion gripped Great Britain in 1940, thousands of foreign nationals were being deported because it was feared they might be enemy spies. They were put on board the HMT Dunera, which had a capacity of 1,600 including the crew. The ship set sail from Liverpool on 10 July 1940, without any of the passengers – who later became known as the 'Dunera Boys' – knowing where they were going. The vessel was crammed with some 2,500 mostly Jewish refugees, aged 16 to 60, including the 20-year-old Henry Böhm, Ruth's cousin. Also on board were genuine prisoners of war, 200 Italian fascists and 251 German Nazis. But the ship was hopelessly overcrowded.

After a 57-day journey in appalling conditions, during which it was hit by a torpedo, the ship's arrival in Australia is regarded as one of the country's greatest influxes of academic and artistic talent. The Dunera was hugely over capacity, and one of the passengers, German-born Peter Eden, later recalled that the men

'....slept on floors and benches and if you wanted to go to the toilet at night, you were walking on bodies. The troops that were guarding us were the worst in the British Army. I remember seeing someone walking off wearing my raincoat and I lost my watch. The Australians asked us where our luggage was but it had already gone overboard.'

The refugees were kept below decks for the whole time apart from 30 minutes each day, and there were just 10 toilets for more than 2,000 people. This gave rise to the need for 'toilet police' who would call up names as vacancies arose. Fresh water was only supplied two or three times a week, and all razors and shaving equipment was confiscated. In addition, many personal possessions belonging to the internees were stolen by some of the ill-disciplined British guards, many of whom were later accused of acts of cruelty and assault.

Peter Eden said that, while in middle of the Irish Sea, a torpedo hit the Dunera 'with a loud bang' but did not detonate. A second torpedo was then fired, but because the waves were so heavy, the ship rose up just as the torpedo passed underneath it. Yet despite these incidents, the Dunera managed to continue its voyage. Another of the passengers, one who had survived a period in Dachau concentration camp before coming to Britain and boarding the ship, said he found an open hatch below decks through which he and fellow internees would breathe fresh air in ten-minute shifts as a respite from the foul stench of so many bodies confined in a dimly lit, confined space for weeks without any ventilation. When this hatch was discovered by the soldiers, who were later described by many as 'the lowest of the lowest', it was sealed shut.

When the ship arrived in Port Melbourne, Australia, on 3 September, many of the internees disembarked, along with the Italian and Nazi prisoners of war. Henry was put on a train to New South Wales where he was interned in Hay Camp along with 2,000 refugees from Germany and Austria. When the vessel finally docked in Sydney on 6 September 1940, an Australian medical officer came on board, and his damning report subsequently led to a court martial of several of the British guards. A senior officer and a sergeant were severely reprimanded, and another soldier was reduced to the ranks, given a 12-month prison sentence and discharged from the army. The most shocking aspect of this whole debacle was not so much the conditions on board but the fact that Jewish refugees had been deported alongside groups of Nazi and Italian fascists.

After questions were asked about the matter in the House of Commons, the British government soon realised the gravity of its mistake and looked for a legitimate reason to bring the deportees back, but in a manner in which the government would not lose face. In her book *Freud's War*, Helen Fry quotes Walter Freud, who later wrote about the Dunera in his unpublished memoirs. He said:

'Although the most essential medicaments were lacking, vital medicines like insulin were thrown overboard when it was discovered that these belonged to the internees. False teeth were removed, destroyed or thrown overboard..., religious artefacts – vestments, prayer books, Bibles and phylacteries were all taken away or torn up. Some vestments which had actually been removed from burning synagogues in Nazi Germany were returned thanks to the interned Chief Rabbi Lt Malouy.'

In 1985, a film starring Bob Hoskins (*The Dunera Boys*) was released which depicts the shocking events that took place aboard the ship. After spending a short time in Hay Camp, Henry was given the choice of remaining in internment or joining the Australian Army. He decided to join up and subsequently spent almost five years in the 8th Employment Division (non-combat) as a private. After being discharged, he went to live with his Aunt Kate in Sydney and, for some time, worked in a delicatessen. In April 1948, Henry met his future wife, Lilly Steiner, and they were married just six months later.

Henry Böhm and Lilly Steiner

My grandfather Arthur Böhm was, by all accounts, a very colourful and gregarious character and definitely something of an enigma who could, I believe, be rather secretive. Over the past 50 years or so, a story has circulated on my mother's side of the family describing in some detail how Arthur had managed to escape from Germany. Sometime in November 1938, following the terrible events of Kristallnacht, Arthur was apparently tipped off by an old school friend that his (Arthur's) name was on a list of Jews soon to be arrested by the Gestapo and deported. Arthur immediately decided that to save himself from arrest, he would have to get out of Germany as soon as possible, so he simply abandoned his wife and Ruth in Breslau and somehow got to Denmark from where he hoped to get a visa to enter the United States. Nothing is known about his movements over the following two months, but we do know that he eventually arrived in Manila on 10 February 1939. No doubt he believed that from there he would be able to get to America.

It is a little known fact that between 1938 and the early 1940s, the president of the Philippines, Manuel L. Quezon, succeeded in rescuing more than a thousand German and Austrian Jews and bringing them to the Philippines at a time when few countries were prepared to take in Jewish refugees. Under the guise of boosting the Philippine economy, Quezon cleverly published a series of classified advertisements inviting Jewish professionals to come to the Philippines. However, one stumbling block appears to have been the refusal of the United States to open up the border. In 1942, Quezon's strategy came to an abrupt end following the Japanese invasion of the Philippines. Although he had managed to save 1,200 Jews from certain death, Quezon died in 1944 in exile in Saranac Lake, New York, his dream of saving at least 10,000 Jews unfulfilled.

Arthur remained in the Philippines until the second half of 1946 when he eventually managed to get to Australia to join his sister, Kate, and brother, George, in Sydney. In a letter to Ruth written in June 1946, he complains bitterly about everyday life in Manila during this turbulent period:

'You wrote about life in Germany but it can't be worse than here – what with food shortages, robberies and pickpockets! If it was possible to steal $100 from my buttoned shirt pocket six months ago then that really is something. But this has happened to me on three separate occasions! There is not one refugee here who could say that he hasn't been affected by robbing or stealing. The Wild West is nothing compared to the Philippines. But in general, the whole world is in a state of unrest because too many arms are in the possession of lawless people. In several provinces here we now have a state of civil war because of the election of a new president. Of course, there are bad elements among his opponents, and so every day we can read in the Manila News about atrocities, people being killed and whole villages being burned.'

Until some years ago, I had always believed the above version of events surrounding Arthur's escape from Germany. Two things have however since led me to question the truth of this story. Firstly, in a conversation with my Aunt Ilse in Sydney in 1994, she told me that this was not exactly how it happened. In fact, she says, her mother, Clara, had come to resent Arthur and would probably not have agreed to go anywhere with him, let alone to the other side of the world. The second thing which appears to cast doubt on this story is something which appears in one of Arthur's letters to Ruth in which he implies that he was trying his best to bring his wife to join him in Manila. In a separate letter from Clara to Ruth written in May 1941, Clara makes her feelings about her estranged husband very clear:

'*The old man (Arthur) is also alive and has even visited Jetta. But apparently, she gave him a good piece of her mind. He cannot forget the letter that you wrote to him either. What you predicted for him seems to have come true because he is still all on his own. He is trying his best to scrape a living but things don't look too rosy for him. Let him do what he likes. I am not interested anymore – those times are long gone. I have become a completely different person now, and everyone says that I even look different. I have noticed this myself because of all the attention (from other men) that I still manage to get.*'

A letter Ruth received from Clara's sister, Erna, in September 1954 contains the following vitriolic remark about Arthur: '*...it takes me a long time to hate someone, but what he has done to my sister is so wicked...*' So Arthur may well have withdrawn money from the family bank account and, true to form, simply put his own interests first in fleeing Germany alone. But I am still unsure whether, as Ruth had always maintained, it can be said that he intentionally 'abandoned' her and her mother. The marriage appeared to be over anyway, and I believe that they had both decided to go their own separate ways.

George Böhm was the only one of Louis and Jenni's sons who had decided to go to university and follow a professional career. He had begun his dentistry studies before the First World War and although he appears to have returned to Katscher briefly once the war was over and perhaps even helped out in the family business, he and his wife, Elfriede, subsequently settled in Gleiwitz where he established his practice in Nicolaistrasse (today, ul. Mikolowska) after he qualified. Following Kristallnacht in 1938, George and Elfriede must have also started to fear for their own safety and that of their son and daughter and soon realised that they needed to get out of Germany as soon as possible. In a letter to Ruth, written in July 1939, George writes:

'I know how difficult it is to get out. We are trying to get to Chile, but whether we will be lucky or not is another matter.'

In fact, it would be another year before they were finally granted an exit visa – not to Chile as they had originally planned – but to Shanghai. It is not clear why there was a last-minute change of destination, but by the time they left for Shanghai on 14 October 1940, many countries had already closed their doors to refugees, and Shanghai may have been the only option still open to them as it was one of the few remaining countries that did not demand a visa.

It has been estimated that at least 17,000 German and Austrian Jews fled to Shanghai between the time that the Nazi persecution of the Jews started in 1933 and 1939 when refugees began to flood into the city in much larger numbers. During the 1930s, Nazi policy had actively encouraged Jewish emigration from Germany, but once the war had started, it became much more difficult to obtain a visa to leave. At first, Shanghai had seemed an unlikely refuge, but when it became clear that most countries in the world were limiting or denying entry to Jews, for many it became the only available choice. Ernest Heppner, who fled Breslau with his mother in 1939, recalls:

'The main thing was to get out of Germany, and really at this point, people did not care where they went, anywhere just to get away from Germany' (Ernest Heppner, USHMM Oral History, 1999).

Arriving in Shanghai in the middle of the Sino-Japanese War that had started in 1937 must have been something of a culture shock, especially for those who had just stepped off a European liner on which they had been served breakfast by uniformed stewards but who now found themselves lining up for lunch in a soup kitchen.

Once the refugees had settled in, finding work proved to be the biggest challenge, and many refugees were forced to rely heavily on charitable relief. Yet despite the dire financial straits which they found themselves in, the majority of German and Austrian Jews did somehow manage. Despite the severe blows to Shanghai's economy dealt by the Sino-Japanese conflict, some of them adapted well, taking advantage of all the opportunities the city had to offer. The Eisfelder family, which had arrived at the end of 1938, opened and operated Café Louis, a popular gathering place for refugees throughout the war years. Others established small factories or cottage industries, set themselves up as doctors or teachers or worked as architects or builders to help transform sections of the bombed-out Hongkou district. By 1940, an area around Chusan Road had become known as 'Little Vienna' on account of its European-style cafés, delicatessens, nightclubs, shops and bakeries.

However, following the Japanese attack on Pearl Harbour in December 1941, George and Elfriede were interned in the now almost-forgotten Lungwha Internment Camp, along with 1,800 other foreigners. Ironically, they had fled Germany for fear of being imprisoned (or worse) simply for being German and Jewish, and here they were now being imprisoned as enemy aliens, although the Japanese had nothing against the Jews. Upon their release, they were forced to live in the so-called Restricted Area for Stateless Refugees in the Hongkou district, which later became known as the 'Shanghai Ghetto'.

Hongkou (Photo Jewish Museum of Maryland)

When Shanghai's refugee population suddenly jumped from about 1,500 at the end of 1938 to nearly 17,000 one year later, the local Jews were overwhelmed and were hard pressed to find the resources to help those families in greatest need. The Committee for Assistance of European Jewish Refugees in Shanghai, formed in 1938 by prominent local Jews turned to the Joint Distribution Committee (JDC) in New York for additional funds. The JDC appropriation rose from $5,000 in 1938 to $100,000 in 1939, but even this substantial increase barely kept up with the mounting demands. By late 1939, more than half of the refugee population required financial help for food or housing.

By the time George and Elfriede had arrived in Shanghai, their son, Henry, was already in Australia, whereas their daughter, Edith, had managed to get to the United States. Edith had married her first husband, Gerhardt Chrzanowski, in December 1937 in Gleiwitz while he was still training to be a psychiatrist in Berlin.

Edith Böhm

However, due to ever-more stringent Nazi regulations, he was forced to suspend his studies and then went to Switzerland where he managed to complete his degree. I believe that Edith eventually joined him in Switzerland. As soon as he had graduated, the couple managed to immigrate to the United States. Edith arrived in New York on 28 May 1940 aboard the SS *Washington*, and Gerhardt joined her one month later.

Initially, life was extremely difficult for them, and the only job Edith was able to get was working as a nanny. By this time, Gerhardt had also found a suitable position, but sometime in 1942, the couple divorced. Edith then moved to Florida where she met her second husband, Jack Whalen, who was from Cleveland, Ohio, and, it is believed, worked in politics. They were married in Fort Lauderdale in February 1944 and eventually settled in Miami where, for many years, Edith worked as a maître d' at a golf country club. Once she had retired and been widowed, George's wife,

Fanny, helped Edith get to Australia in 1984 where she settled in Rose Bay and lived there until her death in May 2006.

We cannot be sure whether George managed to set himself up as a dentist immediately after his arrival in Shanghai or whether this came later. An official certificate of registration to allow him to practice as a dentist is dated December 1943, but this may have been something that had to be renewed annually. However, it was likely that he and Elfriede would have needed to rely on the charity of others to survive during the early months in Shanghai. But life in a country whose culture would have been completely different from what they had been used to in Germany could not have been easy for the couple, but survive they did until, barely two years after their arrival, tragedy struck.

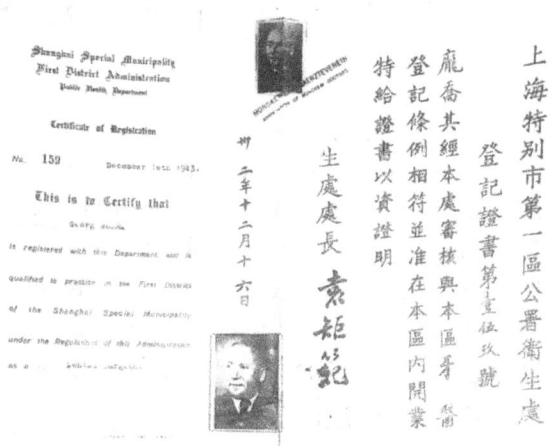

George Böhm's Chinese dental licence

On 10 September 1942, George's wife, Elfriede, died, apparently as a result of a long illness. George was to spend another three years in Shanghai, continuing to practice as a dentist before being granted an entry permit for Australia in 1945.

TRAGEDY AND DESPAIR

Back in Germany as 1941 got underway, instead of enjoying what should have been a relaxing retirement, Louis Böhm was becoming more and more despondent. Three of his four remaining sons had already left Germany (Arthur, Walter and George), as had his daughter, Kate, and his son-in-law, Henry Schweiger. His fourth son, Siegbert, with whom Louis still had some sporadic contact, was living in Berlin at this time – I believe with his partner. Furthermore, his seven grandchildren Ilse, Ruth, Edith, Henry, Margot, Gary and Steffi, whom he had always been so fond of, had also all left. His entire family which had for so many years been the main focus of his life was no longer there. Nor could he be sure whether he would ever see any of them again. As if all this were not enough for an 80-year old man to bear, his wife, Jenni, who had been seriously ill for some time, was now clinging to life by a mere thread. In a heartfelt letter written to his son George in February 1941, Louis reveals the severity of her condition.

'*She is declining from one day to the next. Her whole body is now nothing more than a skeleton, and the open wound is causing her great pain. She eats very little and, in addition, she is often talking nonsense. May the dear God just have mercy on her and take her so that she can be released from her terrible pain. My grief is very deep, but no-one can help me now, only the dear Lord.'*

Jenni died on 17 March 1941 and was buried in the Jewish cemetery in Katscher. We can imagine that there were probably very few mourners at her funeral because her family was no longer there and all but a handful of Jews had already left the area. Louis was now all alone, although his faithful housekeeper Anna Jaschke did remain with him until the very end. As was the case for many other people whose close relatives had already emigrated, letters from abroad came to be the most important thing in their lives. This was also the case for Louis. The joy and relief he felt upon receiving each and every letter from his children and grandchildren is palpable in much of his correspondence. In a letter to his son George written just a few months after Jenni's death, Louis writes:

'I was so delighted to receive your letter of 20th May, and I would like to say thank you to you dear George for so often taking the opportunity to write to your dear father. That is a great comfort to me.'

Because the cost of postage for overseas mail could be quite expensive, it was common for people sending letters from Germany to relatives abroad to enclose a pre-paid reply coupon.

Pre-paid postage coupon

The year 1942 would prove to be one of the most fateful and tragic years in the history of the Böhm family. The Wannsee Conference, which took place on 20 January 1942, was a meeting of senior government officials and Schutzstaffel (SS) leaders and was held in the Berlin suburb of Wannsee. The purpose of the conference, called by the director of the Reich Main Security Office, SS-Obergruppenführer Reinhard Heydrich, was to ensure the co-operation of administrative leaders of the various government departments in the implementation of the 'Final Solution' to the Jewish question, whereby most of the Jews of German-occupied Europe would be deported to Poland and murdered. The conference participants included representatives from several government ministries, including state secretaries from the Foreign Office, the Justice Department, Interior and state ministries and representatives from the SS. During the course of the meeting, Heydrich outlined how European Jews would be rounded up and sent to extermination camps in the so-called 'General Government (the occupied part of Poland), where they would be systematically killed.

The Wannsee Conference was to have dire consequences for all the Jews who had failed to gain an exit visa and were still living in Germany at this time. After having been completely ostracised following the 1933 Race Laws, enduring years of living as second-class citizens and having all their property and civil rights taken away from them, their very lives were now at stake. Clara Böhm was the first member of the family to fall victim to the harsh reality of life for those Jews who had remained in Germany after the Wannsee Conference. Like all other Jewish women at this time, she had been forced to add 'Sara' to her name and to wear a yellow star sewn onto her clothing whenever she left her home. As part of the August 1938 race laws, it had been decreed that by 1 January 1939, all Jewish men and women bearing first names of 'non-Jewish' origin had to add 'Israel' and 'Sara', respectively, to their given names. Furthermore, all German Jews were obliged to carry identity cards that indicated their heritage, and starting in the autumn of 1938, all

Jewish passports had to be stamped with an identifying red letter 'J'.

Elfriede Böhm's passport

Clara was arrested in Breslau sometime around the middle of November and transported to a holding camp in the Grüssau monastery. She remained there until April 1942 when, we believe, she was sent to Theresienstadt in Czechoslovakia. Theresienstadt could best be described as a hybrid concentration camp and ghetto that the SS established during the Second World War in the fortress town of Terezín, located in the Protectorate of Bohemia and Moravia (a German-occupied region of Czechoslovakia). Although Theresienstadt was essentially a feeder camp for Auschwitz and some of the other extermination camps, it also served as a 'retirement settlement' for elderly and prominent Jews, having been set up with the sole intention of misleading their communities and the world at large about the nature of the Final Solution. The conditions in the camp were deliberately engineered to hasten the death of its prisoners, and the ghetto also served an important propaganda role for the Nazis.

The ghetto was established by a transport of Czech Jews in November 1941, with the first German and Austrian Jews arriving between April and June 1942. Dutch and Danish Jews came at the beginning of 1943, and prisoners of a wide variety of nationalities were sent there during the war's final months. It has been estimated that about 33,000 people died in Theresienstadt, mostly from malnutrition and disease. Many prisoners were held there for months or even years before finally being deported to extermination camps and other killing sites, such as Auschwitz and Buchenwald.

The central role played by the camp's Jewish administrators in selecting those to be deported has attracted a great deal of controversy over the years. One of the most notorious of these, Benjamin Murmelstein, had been one of only 17 community rabbis in Vienna in 1938 and was the only one who was still in the city by late 1939. He was an important figure and board member of the Jewish group in Vienna during the early stages of the war, and from 1943 onwards, he was also an *Ältester* (council elder) of the Judenrat (Jewish council) in the Theresienstadt concentration camp. He was the only *Judenältester* to have survived the Holocaust and has been credited with saving the lives of thousands of Jews by assisting in their emigration.

Women's camp, Theresienstadt

But he was also accused of being a Nazi collaborator. Whatever his actions and motivation may have been, the liberation of Theresienstadt did not immediately lead to lasting freedom for Murmelstein, as he was quickly detained by the Czechoslovak government on suspicion of collaboration. But the authorities were unable to build a case against him, and towards the end of 1946, Murmelstein was released and allowed to immigrate to Rome with his family. He was subsequently employed in some kind of administrative capacity in the Vatican and also worked as a salesman for a short time. Although never formally charged, he was unable to salvage his ruined reputation. During his final years, Murmelstein made an effort to restore his reputation. In 1961, he published a memoir of his wartime experiences, *Terezin: Il ghetto-modello di Eichmann*. He also volunteered to stand as a witness at the trial of Adolf Eichmann in Jerusalem but was never called to the stand. He then lived in relative obscurity until he was interviewed by *Shoah* film director Claude Lanzmann in 1975. The Roman Jewish community refused to enrol him in its registers, and when he died in 1989, he was not allowed to be interred next to his wife but was relegated to a plot on the margins of the Jewish cemetery in Rome. His son was also denied the right to recite the *Kaddish* (Jewish mourners' prayer) over his grave.

Out of a total of 155,000 people who were sent to Theresienstadt during the period it operated, some 33,000 died there, and more than 88,000 prisoners were deported to other camps to be murdered. The total number of survivors is estimated to have been around 23,000. Theresienstadt was known for its relatively rich cultural life that included concerts, lectures and clandestine education for children. The fact that it was self-governed by Jews and the large number of 'prominent' Jews imprisoned there were the main reasons cultural life flourished. This spiritual legacy has attracted the attention of scholars and has sparked renewed interest in the ghetto. In the post-war period, a few of the SS perpetrators and Czech guards were put on trial, but Soviet authorities generally forgot about the camp.

We believe that Clara died sometime during May 1942 in Theresienstadt, but in light of the fact that, as was usually the case, no death certificate was ever issued, it is impossible to know for certain how or when she died. Although individual guards often carried out spontaneous killings of individual prisoners, Theresienstadt was not a killing camp as such, and most of the people who met their deaths there died from disease resulting from the poor conditions and food. This was probably what happened to Clara who was aged just 50 at the time of her death.

The second member of the Böhm family to perish during the Holocaust was Siegbert who, as a homosexual and a Jew, had been forced to keep a very low profile and lead a largely secretive life with his partner in Berlin since the mid-1930s. According to a census of 16 June 1933, the Jewish population of Berlin numbered about 160,000. Berlin's Jewish community was the largest in Germany, making up almost a third of all the Jews in the country, but in the face of increasing Nazi persecution, many Jews had already left the city. Berlin's Jewish population fell to about 80,000 as a result of emigration from Nazi Germany between 1933 and 1939, despite the fact that Jews from other parts of Germany also moved into the city during this period. In January 1939, the Gestapo arrested Siegbert and took him to Buchenwald concentration camp where he was briefly detained for questioning before being released. His only crime was that of being Jewish.

The mass deportation of Jews from Berlin to ghettos and killing centres in Eastern Europe took place between October 1941 and April 1943. Assembly points for the deportations were established at synagogues on Levetzow Street and Heidereuter Alley, at the Jewish cemetery on Grosse Hamburger Strasse, and on Rosenstrasse. Sometime later, even the Jewish home for the aged, the community office building, and the Jewish hospital were used as assembly centres. Once enough Jews for an entire transport (usually 1,000 people) had been assembled in these makeshift centres, they were taken to the railway station, the freight yards at Grünewald or sometimes the Anhalter or Putlitz Street train stations. There they were loaded onto passenger rail cars or sometimes into freight cars.

The first deportation took place in October 1941, when 1,000 Jews were transported to the Łódź ghetto in Poland. By January 1942, about 10,000 Jews had been deported from Berlin to ghettos in Eastern Europe, mainly Łódź, Riga, Minsk and Kovno. Elderly Jews from Berlin were deported to Theresienstadt in 1942 and 1943. Beginning in 1942, Jews were deported from Berlin directly to the killing centres primarily to Auschwitz-Birkenau. The majority of the remaining Jews in Berlin had been transported by the end of April 1943. In total, more than 60,000 Jews were deported from Berlin, and hundreds of others committed suicide rather than submit to the deportations. Siegbert was arrested by the Gestapo on 2 March 1943 at his lodgings in Oranienstrasse and was sent on Transport No. 32 to Auschwitz where he was almost certainly gassed. He was just 53 years old.

The tragic fate of Louis Böhm, the last remaining member of the family in Katscher, marks a low point in our story. In a letter to his son George that Louis had written in August 1939, he reports that he had sold the house in Thrömerstrasse for much less than what it was worth but that he and Jenni would be allowed to live there for the rest of their lives for an annual rent of 960 Reichsmarks. He had also rented out part of the upper floor to Paul Wiener (a family friend) for an annual rent of 420 Reichsmarks. After his wife, Jenni, died in March 1941, Louis decided to stay on in the house, along with Anna Jaschke, his housekeeper. He appears to have held some kind of administrative role at the time connected with the Jewish community in Katscher and the surrounding area, but for a man now in his early 80s, this job was obviously becoming a burden, as is clear from a letter he wrote to his son George:

'"Our parish has now given me two extra external people, which means that I now have to look after ten people. So I have a lot more paperwork to do than I had before. I have to send various letters, etc. to the district office in Gleiwitz and, as of 1 June, these will have to go to Breslau. I have already sent a request to the Reichsvereinigung (national administration) in Berlin asking them to release me from the post in view of my age. But they won't let me go and have asked me to stay in the position even if there is just one member remaining.'

There is only scant information about how Louis occupied himself between the time Jenni died and when he finally left Katscher for good. But we already know that the house was acquired by a Polish family in 1945 and that it had stood empty and in a state of poor disrepair for most of the preceding two years. But sometime during 1944, it was briefly occupied by German officers in charge of a small military unit based in the town. This means that we can assume that Louis finally left the villa in Thrömerstrasse sometime early in 1943. This would appear to be the case because nothing more is known about his whereabouts until his arrest in Oppeln in April of that year. It is not entirely clear why Louis went to Oppeln (today, Opole, Poland) some 80 kilometres north of Katscher. However, following the Wannsee Conference in January 1942, the Nazis had initiated a major roundup of Jews throughout Upper Silesia and were keen to get all the Jews assembled together in the three main centres of Breslau, Kattowitz and Oppeln, thus making it easier logistically for the mass deportations which were to follow. So in all probability, the authorities had ordered Louis to go to Oppeln, and he would have had little choice but to comply.

On 21 May 1943, Rolf Günther, Adolf Eichmann's deputy, informed all local police forces that Heinrich Himmler had ordered that all deportations of Jews from the Greater Reich and the Protectorate to the East and to Theresienstadt were to be completed by 30 June 1943. This new order also applied to several groups of Jews whose deportation had previously been postponed. These included mainly sick and infirm people, Jews who were still employed in slave labour for the war industry, and employees of the *Reichsvereinigung der Juden* (National Association of the Jews). The only exemptions allowed were those people who were married to non-Jews. The regulations also laid down guidelines as to how the deportations themselves were to be carried out. In the case of smaller transports of up to 400 people, special carriages hitched to regular trains were to be used. The deportation of the Jewish inhabitants of Oppeln began in earnest on 13 November 1942, and on that day, Transport No. 18/1 left with 56 Jews from Oppeln, Głubczyce and Bytom bound for the Theresienstadt ghetto.

On 11 December 1942, another transport took 53 people from the Opole Regierungsbezirk to the Theresienstadt ghetto. Only seven people survived from this group. The fifth transport, No. 18/5, consisting of 46 Jews, departed from Oppeln for Theresienstadt on 21 April 1943, and on the train were Louis Böhm and, it is believed, his housekeeper, Anna Jaschke. It is known that only 11 people out of this group survived.

The last Jews from Oppeln, along with five Jews from Ratibor, were deported to Theresienstadt on the sixth transport that left on 30 June 1943.

Exactly how Louis met his end has always been the subject of some conjecture within the family. However, the story that everyone seems to have subscribed to is as follows. At the time of his arrest, Louis was aged 83 and, according to Anna, was already a sick man.

She claims that he had a stoma which must have been a consequence of some kind of bowel surgery, although there is no mention of this in any of his letters. During the journey of around 450 kilometres from Oppeln to Theresienstadt (Terezin) in Czechoslovakia, it became necessary for Louis's colostomy bag to be changed. Anna Jaschke had apparently decided out of sheer loyalty to Louis to travel with him on the transport even though she was not actually Jewish. Her urgent request to have the colostomy bag changed was denied, and Louis subsequently died, presumably of septicaemia, before the train had reached its final destination. The above account apparently came from Anna Jaschke herself who somehow survived the transport and, after the war, settled in a small town in Bavaria.

Shortly before completing this book, a researcher based in Poland who had been helping me with a number of local searches lodged a direct enquiry with the records department of the Terezin museum in Czechoslovakia. It was able to confirm that Louis was in fact killed in Theresienstadt in July 1944 and referred us to an entry in the Yad Vashem central database of victims who were murdered during the Shoah or Holocaust. This database is based on extensive lists prepared by the German National Archives for the period from 1933 to 1945. Louis is indeed listed in this archive, and all the details relating to his date and place of birth, place of residence and date of arrest and transport No. are absolutely correct. The final entry in the listing for Louis confirms that he was murdered on 23 July 1944 in Theresienstadt. The URL link to the relevant entry in the Yad Vashem database can be found in the References section at the end of the book.

This new information regarding Louis's death obviously raises the question of how the original story of his dying on the train originated. There is of course no way we can answer this question with any certainty so long after the event, but we can perhaps allow ourselves a little reasoned speculation. We know that Anna had worked for Louis and Jenni for more than 25 years and that she had always been completely loyal to both of them. In light of this loyalty, it is therefore quite feasible that she had volunteered to accompany Louis on the transport from Oppeln to Theresienstadt. We also know that Anna survived the war and subsequently settled in southern Germany, but I find it difficult to believe that a non-Jewish person could have travelled on a train transporting Jews to a concentration camp and then, when the train had reached its final destination, simply have been released by saying that she was not Jewish. Perhaps Anna fabricated her story to spare the feelings of whoever it was with whom she first shared this account of Louis's final journey. The other aspect of her story which I find a little puzzling relates to Louis Böhm's medical condition. If, as Anna had reported, Louis had a stoma, it is highly unlikely that he would have survived more than a few months in Theresienstadt where the living conditions and general level of hygiene were known to have been horrific. If it is indeed the case that Louis was murdered in July 1944 (and I am inclined to believe the official records), then he must have been in reasonably good health, which leads me to question the veracity of the stoma story.

In February 1944, the SS embarked on a so-called beautification campaign to prepare the Theresienstadt ghetto for an important Red Cross visit later that year. But the main objective of course was to fool the outside world into believing that those Jews who had been 'resettled' in Theresienstadt were leading a happy and fulfilled life in a pleasant environment. Many prominent prisoners and Danish Jews were even re-housed in private, almost luxurious quarters. In fact, it was the Danish government that had asked the Red Cross to inspect the camp. The streets were renamed and cleaned, and sham shops and a school were set up. The SS ordered the prisoners to participate in an increasing number of cultural activities to create the impression that there were always many interesting things to do in the camp. But as part of the extensive clean-up preparations, 7,500 people were sent to Auschwitz during May. The transports consisted mainly of sick, elderly and disabled people who would have had no place in what the Germans were hoping to portray as an ideal Jewish settlement. For the remaining prisoners, conditions improved somewhat. According to one survivor:

'The summer of 1944 was the best time we had ever had in Terezín. Nobody gave any thought to any new transports.'

On 23 June 1944, the Red Cross visitors were led on a tour through the so-called Potemkin village. Predictably, they did not notice anything that raised their concerns, and the ICRC representative, Maurice Rossel, subsequently reported that, as far as he was concerned, no-one had been deported from Theresienstadt. Rabbi Leo Baeck, a well-known spiritual leader in the ghetto, recalls, 'The effect on our morale was devastating. We all felt forgotten and forsaken.' In August and September, a propaganda film that became known as *'Der Führer schenkt den Juden eine Stadt'* (*The Führer Gives the Jews a City*) was shot but was never distributed. In the light of the inconsistencies in the Anna Jaschke story and the fact that there was no alternative explanation available at the time of writing, I believe that we must now accept that Louis was killed on 23 July 1944 in Theresienstadt.

PEACE AT LAST AND A NEW LIFE

After having been interned for almost two years, Ruth Böhm was finally released from the Rushen camp on the Isle of Man on 10 March 1942. Her release papers indicate that she was sent to live and work in Salford in the north of England where there would have been a great deal of heavy industry at the time. However, she did not stay long in Salford, because by August of that year, she had already decided to move to Harrogate in Yorkshire. I believe that there were two conditions attached to her release. Firstly, she was expected to contribute towards the war effort, which in her case meant working in an aircraft assembly factory. Secondly, she would be expected to put her young son, Peter, who was barely 18 months old at the time, into care from Monday to Friday each week while she trained and worked as a machine operator. To be forced to surrender her child into the arms of strangers every week for two long years must have been deeply traumatising for Ruth, as her son had barely left her side since he was born. Apparently, this was also a distressing experience for Peter who believes to this day that this extended period of being repeatedly ripped away from his mother probably affected him for life. This was also around the time Ruth was to receive the last-ever letter from her mother, Clara, who, just two months later, would be dead. By this time, Clara would probably have realized that she would never see either of her daughters again, nor would she ever be able to hold her grandson, Peter.

'The longing that I feel is indescribable. So I am happy that you and the child are both healthy. And I reassure myself with the thought, Ruth, that you have become such a loving mother. It hurts me so much that I cannot be there to share your joy with your child. When you were that age, you looked exactly like little Peter. I would so love to see him.'

In spite of her shortcomings, my mother could be very tough when circumstances required it. To this day, I am full of admiration for the fortitude, determination and sheer will to carry on that she must have found within herself during this very difficult period in her life. She was a young woman all alone with a small child in a foreign country where she still did not fully understand the language and customs of the people around her. But somehow she survived and in spite of impossibly adverse circumstances, she was, I believe, a good mother to Peter.

The following year, Ruth appears to have moved to the other side of the Pennines and, in 1943, was living in Leeds, Yorkshire. We must assume that she was still working, as this had been a strict condition of her release from internment. There was also a new man in her life. Letters left by my mother when she died reveal that sometime during late 1943 or early 1944, she had had an affair with a man called Harold Storey who worked as a bailiff for the Earl of Harewood on his vast country estate near Leeds. Harold Storey was also the landlord of the Harewood Arms pub and was an accomplished organist who would often entertain a close circle of friends in the private church on the estate after he had closed up the pub. We believe that the couple probably met at a charity event in aid of Jewish refugees, but we do not know how long the affair lasted, although it was clearly complicated by the fact that Harold was already married with children. In spite of this, I think that it must have been an intense love affair because, right up until the time of her death, Ruth had held on to a handwritten picture postcard that Harold had sent to her when they were no longer together. The picture on the front of the postcard is of Harewood Church, which stood on the grounds of Harewood estate and, as a private place of worship, would have been off-limits to members of the general public and would therefore have been the perfect place for the two of them to meet in secret. As a trusted employee of the estate, Harold would have had unfettered access to the building, which was finally decommissioned as a church in the early 1970s. The brief message on the back of this postcard provides, I think, a touching insight into what must have been a passionate and spiritual liaison:

'In loving and glorious memory of the happiest day – 14 June 1943 – of your visit. You will recognise where we prayed together. Keep this little card Ruth darling – as time goes on, it will help to keep fresh the lovely memories of that perfect, heavenly day. God bless you, Harold.'

But after a matter of some months, it was all over. In a poignant last letter to Ruth written in July 1945, sometime after the affair had ended, Harold says:

'I agree with you in your decision about us, but at the time it was difficult for me to accept it. I am now living at home with my wife and children and doing all I can to make them happy. I will never forget the months we were together and I know you will not either. Life is difficult but I am glad that you have not regretted knowing me.'

This letter would seem to confirm that the two of them were actually together as a couple for a while and that Harold may even have left his wife before going back to her. I believe that the main reason Ruth decided to end the affair was that she had been confronted by Harold's wife who had found out about her husband's infidelity. She threatened to report Ruth to the police and told her that, because she was Jewish and an enemy alien, she would almost certainly be sent back to Germany where terrible things were bound to happen to her. Undoubtedly very naïve at this time, my mother would certainly have believed this complete fabrication to be true, so she decided that she would have to leave the area immediately.

It is not known exactly how Ruth managed to end up in South Wales, sometime after ending the affair with Harold. But we do know that she was certainly in the Cardiff area working as a domestic help before the war ended at the beginning of September 1945. It could be that she had responded to a job advertisement, or maybe she knew someone within the Jewish network, which was, and still is particularly strong in the north of England, who had contacts and had helped her make the move. Scores of informal Jewish networks sprang up across the United Kingdom following the end of the war to help the thousands of refugees who had found themselves stranded in the country, unable to return to their homeland. One such network that was particularly active was based in the town of Merthyr Tydfil where a Jewish community had existed since the 1820s. It is possible that Ruth decided to move to South Wales because she either knew or had been introduced to someone in this area through her network of contacts. But I believe that it was actually in the city of Cardiff, situated just 20 miles south of Merthyr Tydfil, where she first met my father, George Vincent.

He had worked as a coal miner for many years, as this was the main industry in South Wales at that time. However, after losing two fingers in an accident while working underground, he was given a compensation payment by the National Coal Board, and with this money, he bought a dilapidated shack on a small plot of land on a bleak hillside in Pennybank, Fochriw, which is situated near the town of Bargoed. As he had always had good practical skills, he apparently managed to transform the shack into a cosy little home which he subsequently named 'Dan-y-Bryn'. Both his parents were living in Cardiff at this time, and this probably explains why George was also there. I believe that he may have been looking for a housekeeper, as he was living alone and may even have advertised the job. So it is possible that Ruth had responded to this advertisement. We will never know for sure, but she did agree to go live with George in Pennybank, initially as his housekeeper.

George, Ruth, Peter and Mervyn, 1947

But as my father had always been something of a womaniser when he was younger, the inevitable happened, and Ruth's role quickly changed from housekeeper to live-in lover. At this time, George was still married but separated from his third wife Maud who had refused to grant him a divorce. Just a year later, my older brother Mervyn was conceived, and by then, Ruth had obviously decided that her being a foreign woman with two young children meant that her best option would be to marry George, although he was 28 years older than she. In a letter sent to Ruth in July 1946, her Aunt Erna Heymann writes:

'It was a great surprise to hear that you are going to get married. I am very, very glad darling because my greatest worry was always that I might have to help you and Peter. You wrote me only that your future husband's name is George and that he is a fitter. Anyway, I wish you all the luck. You will be alright with him in Australia as you will be with a British subject so it will be easy for you to emigrate as they want British people over there.'

The above extract from Erna's letter would seem to suggest that Ruth was intending to immigrate to Australia with George to join the rest of her family. Erna was of course right when she says that being married to a British subject would have made emigration much easier. But it is questionable whether my father would have ever seriously considered going to Australia. He already had a grown-up daughter by his second wife and was now approaching the age of 60. He may have wanted to give Ruth the impression that he was seriously considering emigration just to placate her. In June 1946, Ruth received a letter from her father, Arthur, in Manila who also had strong views about whom she should marry.

'I want to give you my frank opinion about mastering your own future, either by marrying a good man or by going to Australia. I don't know who you have in mind, but if it is a man who 1. Is in good economic conditions – that means that he has his own property and a safe job for some years to come; 2. has a good reputation and an honest character, 3 suitable for you in terms of appearance and is no older than 45 years, then this is the kind of man you should marry, as a woman with a child. Of course life in Australia would also be attractive because of the nice climate and the fact that you would be reunited with your father and your relatives. But for your sake and Peter's, it is up to you now to decide what to do. But I have given you my fatherly advice anyway. I expect (to receive) details about the man that you intend to marry. After this, I will give you my final opinion.'

I think it is fair to say that my father would have failed miserably to meet any of the criteria that Arthur lays down in the above letter. Ruth had always seemed to favour her mother anyway, so it is hardly surprising that she chose to completely ignore his advice and that she and George were finally married in July 1949.

SANCTUARY AND RENEWAL

As Ruth was setting up home with George Vincent on a bleak hillside in South Wales, the Schweigers and the Böhms were building a new life for themselves on the other side of the world in Australia. A letter that Ruth received from her cousin Gary Schweiger in July 1946 gives us a brief insight into how well this branch of the family was doing in the New World:

'We are usually kept informed about your doings (sic) by Henry who is still in the army and is naturally dying to get out. It should not be long with him now. Uncle George is happy here in Sydney, so at least someone in the family has caught up again. How is your little boy? The Australian climate would do him a world of good. Well perhaps you could enable it to come out here in the not too distant future. We expect your father anytime soon. He is only waiting for a ship. It won't be easy for him to start again, but he still feels young enough I guess.'

Ruth had always been close to all her cousins, but she and Henry seemed to have had a special relationship, so we can assume that they also kept in regular contact with each other during the difficult post-war period. By a strange irony, many years later when they were no longer in touch, Henry chose to call one of his daughters Wendy Ruth, and Ruth named one of her sons Kenneth Henry.

Arthur finally arrived in Sydney in the autumn of 1946 and was met at the quay by Steffi's husband, Walter Freeman. Apparently Arthur swaggered down the gangplank, immaculately dressed as usual, and his very first words to Walter were as follows: 'Where can I find a good woman in this town?' As a matter of fact, he did manage to find a good woman rather quickly in the person of a certain Mrs Pengelly but, as a 61-year old man, starting a new life in a new country was certainly not going to be easy. Three years later, it would appear that tensions had already begun to emerge between Arthur and the Schweigers, and it is clear that he was not finding it so easy to adapt to the Australian way of life. In a letter to Ruth written in November 1949, he does not hold back from expressing his views about his extended family:

'I don't want to jump the gun and congratulate you before you let me know the news yourself (presumably about my brother Robert, who was born on 23rd October 1949). *But then I will be very happy. Gerdt (Gary) Schweiger has recently become a father – to a girl – mother and child are doing OK, but it was very difficult. Gerdt bought a shoe shop in Cooma – 300 miles from Sydney and is doing well and is now earning twice as much as his father. Kate has a good life, and every Saturday she goes on a long drive in her new Ford Prefect ... but without me. They say old friends take priority. So, I will just have to make my own way and find my joy in Nature. I have never known such a quiet life, but you can get used to anything. It's impossible to communicate with these Australians. These people don't want that. People make friends with you and say, 'Hello, lovely day today isn't it? Are you going to the races? Good luck.' ... and that is all. Even in the factory canteen you can observe how people dissociate themselves from foreigners. I always have to sit on my own, but the food still tastes good.'*

In this extract, there is no mistaking Arthur's envy and disappointment that other members of the family were doing much better than he was. Although he had been unable to practise as a dentist, George had managed to set up a successful dental laboratory in Sydney, whilst Kate and Henry were expanding their thriving shoe business in Maroubra. Yet three years after his arrival in Sydney, Arthur was still working in a factory and was obviously finding it extremely difficult to make friends and fit in.

Henry Schweiger outside his Maroubra shop

In a letter written in November 1952, Arthur once again speaks in somewhat disparaging terms about the Schweigers.

'Uncle George is fine and is working hard. He has a practice in the city, and Fanny (George's second wife) is working as a book-keeper in a government job. I see him almost every week, but I rarely see the Schweigers since I don't really like Henry. He is no friend of our family. I have heard nothing from Uncle Walter for two years. I wrote to him quite often but never got a reply.'

By the time that the Second World War had ended in 1945, the Hitler dictatorship had imposed an extremely heavy toll on both the first and second generations of the Böhm family. Within the space of just four years, both Louis and Jenni had died in addition to their son Siegbert and their daughters-in-law Clara und Elfriede. But there was also some good news. Between 1944 and 1948, two weddings in Australia signalled the expansion of the third generation of the Böhm family. Gary married Joyce Watson, and his sister, Steffi, married Walter Friedlander (Freeman). In 1947, Steffi and Walter's daughter Susan was born, and Gary and Joyce's first child, Katryn, was born in 1949. At about the same time, Henry and Kate were able to buy their own house in Maroubra Bay. Meanwhile in Palestine, having divorced Ze'ef Yoffe in 1938, Ilse and her second husband, Günther Hirsch, celebrated the birth of their son, Ronny, in 1945.

Gary Schweiger and Joyce Watson

Two years later, the Hirsch family moved into a small apartment in Kiryat Eliyahu, Haifa. Günther was working as an executive chef for Zim, an Israeli shipping line at the time and had to spend long periods away at sea. Ronny enjoyed a normal childhood until 1956 when the Sinai war broke out, leading to the family having to spend long periods in a bunker. Following this traumatic experience, Ronny apparently developed a stutter which was to stay with him for some time. After much cajoling from Arthur who, for years, had insisted on regularly sending the family the jobs section of the *Sydney Morning Herald* in an attempt to persuade them to come to Australia, Günther and Ilse finally relented and, along with their son Ronny, emigrated in May 1957. However, Tamar and Gidon, who were both in the army at the time, remained in Israel.

I believe that, even in the early 1950s, my mother, Ruth, still harboured a desire to emigrate to Australia to be finally reunited with the rest of the Böhm family. But by 1952, she already had three sons by George (Mervyn, Robert and me), so she was now a mother of four boys. As has already been stated, I do not believe that my father had any intention or desire to go to Australia and because he now had three sons of his own, he would simply not have allowed Ruth to go alone with us children. So I think that for my mother, that particular avenue would now be closed off for good. In fact, she was to remain in the United Kingdom until her death in 1977 at the age of 59. But Ruth did manage to keep up a sporadic correspondence with her father, Arthur, until 1954 when something happened that would result in her cutting him out of her life for good.

It is clear that, even as a young man, Arthur was extremely bad at handling money, and now that he was approaching the age of 65, this aspect of his behaviour had apparently not changed. In virtually every one of his letters, he complains about not having enough money or talks about some money-making scheme that he had dreamt up to improve his financial situation.

Following the end of the Second World War, the German government set up an organisation whose task was to compensate survivors of the war who had been harmed physically or emotionally by their experiences (*Reichsbund für Kriegsbeschädigte*). In 1954, Arthur decided to make a claim on the basis that he had been damaged emotionally by the death of his wife during the Holocaust. He hired a lawyer in Hamburg to handle the case on his behalf but needed three critical documents before his claim for financial compensation could be considered. He was asked to produce a death certificate for Clara along with signed statements from both of his daughters, presumably corroborating his claim that they had not heard from their mother since 1942. In a letter written in August 1954, he makes his appeal:

'About my claim for economic harm with the restitution unit in Mainz - they would now like to be testified from my children that they have heard nothing of Clara since 1942 when the Gestapo took her away from our home in Kronprinzenstrasse 11. I send you enclosed one testification (sic) which you kindly have to sign with your name – no need for this name to be testified by a solicitor. I must get the same from Ilse. It is not so easy to get money from the German government but I, as a war-damaged veteran, have priority. Furthermore, my age makes my case urgent. I am now a 69-year old disabled pensioner.'

For Ruth, this was the final straw. She had always believed that Clara had died because Arthur had simply abandoned her and her mother in 1939 and just decided to save himself, leaving the country literally overnight. Now her father was asking for her help to extract money from the German government by exploiting Clara's death. She never replied to the letter, and as far as I know, she never had any further contact with him for the rest of his life, although Arthur did write to her once more in February 1960 simply to wish her all the best for her birthday. It is possible that Ilse did actually return her testimonial to Arthur, as she had always been very supportive of him and would probably have been keen to assist him with his claim. However, he was still faced with another problem. A search that I conducted as part of the preparation for this book turned up the original document from August 1954 requesting a death certificate for Clara Böhm. But the official response from the central administration department in Berlin states that because there was no proof of death on record for Clara, a death certificate could not be issued. To my knowledge, therefore, Arthur never received any additional money from the German government, although he did continue to draw his basic German pension of seven pounds and 13 shillings. This whole exercise probably cost him a great deal of money, and he had lost a daughter in the process.

The year 1954 was also marked by another important event which should be mentioned here. Ilse, along with her second husband Günther Hirsch and their young son Ronny visited Europe in July of that year, and in addition to travelling to Holland and Germany, they also went to South Wales to visit Ruth, George and their four children who were now living in Newbridge, Monmouthshire. The two sisters had not seen each other for 20 years (Ilse had immigrated to Palestine in 1934) and had had virtually no contact during that time. They had based themselves in the north of England because Günther was working for a shipping line at the time and had presumably managed to get the family a free passage to the United Kingdom aboard a ship which had docked at the port of Middlesborough. In a letter written to Ruth while Ilse and her family were in Europe, Ilse outlines her travel plans.

'We will be in London in about two weeks' time, and we will definitely come to see you then. We will only be there for two days, but it will be quicker to get to you from there than from Middlesborough. You can write to me in English if it is easier for you. I can understand and speak English reasonably well, but I can't write it without mistakes. I only speak German to my husband and Hebrew to my children. This might sound funny to you, but Israel is such a strange country and, although I have lived there for 20 years, I have never really settled in.'

It is interesting that Ilse mentions that she never really felt at home in Israel. In fact, just three years later, as stated above, Ilse, Günther and Ronny immigrated to Australia to join the rest of the family. However, Ilse's daughter, Tamar, stayed behind and did not leave Israel until 1974. I have a vague recollection of Ilse's visit to our home in Newbridge in 1954, although I was only about three years of age at the time. I remember meeting Ronny and receiving lots of presents wrapped up in neat little packages. Many years later, when I was living in Sydney, Ilse talked briefly about her visit to South Wales. She said that she had been shocked and saddened to find her sister living in such poverty, which she felt was in stark contrast to the lavish surroundings that they had been used to as children. There is no doubt that we were a poor family, living as we did in a council house on a large working-class estate in this depressed area of Wales where virtually every man of working age was employed in the coal mines. I have often reflected on the fact that if my mother had gone to Australia to join the rest of her family following the end of the Second World War, she would have enjoyed a much more prosperous and happy life than the often impoverished existence she ultimately ended up with. One of the last things she said as she lay dying in hospital was, 'I never had much luck throughout my life.'

I would now like to return briefly to the subject of Arthur and his claim for compensation from the German government. As stated above, he wrote to Ilse and Ruth on 19 August 1954 asking for their help to support his application. When Ruth and Ilse met in South Wales during the previous month – probably around 23 July, judging by the extract from Ilse's letter above, they were not yet aware of Arthur's request. I do not believe that my mother and Ilse had any further contact with each other after their reunion, which I find strange, as they had only just found each other after a silence of 20 years. I am convinced that the reason for this was that they fell out the following month after disagreeing about Arthur's compensation claim. In fact, as far as I know, that there was no further contact again until Ruth eventually managed to trace her sister through the Red Cross in 1976, just a year before she (Ruth) died.

By 1955, most of the members of what had now become the Australian branch of the Böhm family were doing well (excluding Arthur of course). In the ten years that had elapsed since the end of the Second World War, most of them had started new families, embarked on new careers, and bought houses and were no doubt enjoying their new lives in what was often referred to at that time as 'the land of plenty'. But then tragedy struck the family yet again when, on 8 August of that year, Kate's husband, Henry Schweiger, died suddenly, and just four months later, her daughter, Steffi, also died. Apparently, Steffi had always been sickly as a child and had suffered ongoing health problems for most of her life. But she had finally succumbed to breast cancer and was just 31 years old. She had previously had a partial mastectomy, and when the family was told that she would have to have the second breast removed and that she would not have long to live, Henry apparently suffered a fatal heart attack. To have lost both her husband and daughter within such a short period must have been a terrible blow for Kate, who had already suffered the loss of both her parents, one of her brothers and her sister-in-law during the Holocaust. But she still had her brothers George and Arthur, her son, Gary, and no fewer than five grandchildren by that time, so we can imagine that this must have been some small comfort for her. It is not clear whether she still had any contact with her other remaining brother Walter and his daughter, Margot, and her husband who were now settled in Lima.

Losing his wife, Steffi, under such tragic circumstances must also have shaken Walter to the core. The couple had been together for just 11 years, and he was now faced with the prospect of having to raise two young children without their mother. However, Kate quickly pitched in to help wherever she could and became almost like a second mother to her grandchildren Susan and Stephen, even though she must have still been grieving the loss of her daughter and husband. Shortly after arriving from Israel in 1957, Ilse, Günther and Ronny moved into Kate's house in Maroubra Bay, Sydney, where Walter was also living with his two young children. But just a few months later, Ilse and Günther separated, and Walter, Ilse and the children moved out of Kate's house and set up home together in a flat nearby. Ilse and Günther were divorced in 1963, and in January of the following year, she and Walter were married.

We have now reconstructed, as far as has been possible, the story of the first, second and third generations of the Böhm family, starting in 1860 and continuing up to the middle of the 1950s. Although clearly incomplete in places, I feel that the above account does at least provide us with some insight into what the family experienced during the Holocaust and the post-war era and what motivated them to make some of the decisions they did. Of course, the main focus in the above narrative has been the escape, survival and the progress of the family towards a better life in a different country. The Böhms were Jewish emigrants who were forced to flee a fascist regime where they had become reviled as non-citizens and would undoubtedly have been subjected to even more persecution, humiliation and probably death if they had chosen to stay in the country of their birth. But we should not allow ourselves to forget what the Böhms were forced to turn their backs on when they made what must have been a difficult decision to leave Germany forever.

Every member of the family was born and brought up in Upper Silesia, the easternmost region of Germany until 1945 when the borders were changed. Because of its close proximity to Eastern Europe, Silesia had always been a unique part of Germany with its own dialect, customs, ethnic mix and traditions, and there can be little doubt that every member of the Böhm family who was forced to leave their homeland would have done so with a heavy heart and a sense of deep regret.

So far, we have focused mainly on what the family gained by leaving their homeland and making a fresh start in another country. However, I believe that we must now look at what the family actually had to give up as a result of their forced emigration from the land of their birth. We will also explore in some detail the horrors that befell this part of Upper Silesia early in 1945, the fall of Breslau, Gleiwitz, and Katscher and the dramatic transformation that Upper Silesia has gone through since the end of the Second World War.

PART II

DESTRUCTION, INVASION AND RENEWAL

THE SHATTERING OF A SILESIAN DREAM

This part of the book will begin with a brief history of Silesia and the Böhm's hometown of Katscher. However, the cities of Breslau and Gleiwitz were also home to several members of the Böhm family prior to 1942 and therefore represent an important part of their lives during this period. It would, I feel, be remiss of me not to give a short account of the terrible events that unfolded in Breslau and Gleiwitz in the spring of 1945. This section will conclude with a short overview of the dramatic changes that Silesia has experienced since 1945, and we will also explore those aspects of traditional Silesian life that have survived since this beautiful region of Central Europe became part of Poland in 1945.

The Province of Upper Silesia was established as part of the Free State of Prussia in 1919 and was eventually divided into two administrative regions, namely Kattowitz and Oppeln. From 1919 until 1938, the provincial capital was Oppeln, and from 1941 to 1945, the capital was Kattowitz. Other major towns in the region included Beuthen, Gleiwitz, Hindenburg, Neisse, Ratibor and Auschwitz. In 1925, Upper Silesia occupied an area of 3,746 square miles and had a total population of 1.4 million people. Between the years of 1938 and 1941, the region was reunited with Lower Silesia and was renamed the Province of Silesia. The earliest exact census figures for the region date from 1819 when a total of 561,203 people were registered as living in this part of Germany. The ethnic breakdown of the population at that time was as follows:

Poles: 377,100 (67.2%)

Germans: 162, 600 (29%)

Moravians: 12,000 (2.1%)

Czechs: 1,600 (0.3%)

Approximately 1.4% of the total population (i.e. 8,000 people) were Jewish.

However, the population would more than double during the next five decades, reaching more than 1.2 million by 1867, including 742,000 Poles and 457,000 Germans. It is clear that this whole area had been predominately Polish in character for many years. Between 1919 and 1921, three Silesian uprisings occurred amongst the Polish-speaking population of Upper Silesia, culminating in the Battle of Annaberg, which took place in 1921. Following this conflict, which had shown little sign of abating, it was decided that a plebiscite (referendum) should be held asking people to choose whether they wanted to continue to belong to Germany or to become part of Poland. The result of the vote, which took place on 20 March 1921, was unequivocal. A clear majority of 60 per cent of the population voted to remain as part of Germany, whereas only 40 per cent voted in favour of becoming part of Poland.

When the Nazis came to power in 1933, the terms of the German-Polish Accord of 1921 were strictly adhered to. One of the stipulations of the treaty was that equal civil rights were to be guaranteed for all inhabitants of Upper Silesia. A prominent politician at the time, Franz Bernheim, succeeded in convincing the League of Nations to force Nazi Germany to abide by the accord by filing the so-called Bernheim Petition. Accordingly, in September 1933, the Nazi government suspended nearly all antisemitic discrimination laws that had already been imposed and exempted the province from any such future decrees until the accord expired in 1937. This explains why everyday life for Jewish people living in Breslau, Gleiwitz and the surrounding area between 1933 and 1937 was generally more comfortable, as they were subjected to significantly less humiliation and persecution than were those Jews living in other parts of Germany.

Following the invasion of Poland in September 1939, the Polish part of Upper Silesia, which included the industrial city of Kattowitz, was directly annexed into the Province of Silesia. This new territory then became part of the Kattowitz administration. From September 1939 onwards, German occupation forces launched a campaign of brutal repression against the Polish population of eastern Upper Silesia. This initiative of targeted persecution was based on lists drawn up before the war that had identified those Poles who had been politically active. A large number of arrests followed during October and November as part of the initiative that became known as *Intelligenzaktion Schlesien* that was directed against Polish intellectuals, many of whom subsequently perished in the prison camps the Nazis had set up throughout Poland. One of these so-called Polish camps (*Polenlager*) was actually established in Katscher in one of the buildings that was later to become part of the Schaeffler factory. A second wave of arrests came in April and May 1940 during the *AB Aktion*. One of the harshest centres of oppression and torture was the Mikolowska Street prison in Kattowitz where people were reported to have been routinely murdered by the Germans using the guillotine.

Around the same time, the Polish population was systematically expelled from the eastern parts of Upper Silesia, as this area was now occupied by the Germans and had become part of the General Government of Poland. Between 1939 and 1942, around 40,000 Poles were forcibly driven out of the region. Ethnic Germans from

Volhynia and the Baltic countries were then settled in their place in the urban areas of Upper Silesia. Between 1939 and 1943, more than 230,000 ethnic Germans were relocated to the Polish territories of eastern Upper Silesia and the Wartheland. The death toll among the Polish population in Upper Silesia at the hands of the Germans during this brutal period of ethnic cleansing is estimated to have reached at least 25,000.

In 1941, Silesia was again divided into the provinces of Upper and Lower Silesia. Kattowitz in the former Autonomous Silesian Voivodeship of pre-war Poland was made the capital of Upper Silesia rather than the much smaller town of Oppeln. The German province of Upper Silesia was subsequently conquered by the Soviet Red Army between February and the end of March 1945 during the Upper Silesian Offensive at the end of the Second World War. The post-war Potsdam Agreement then handed over the entire region to the People's Republic of Poland, and today, the territory lies within the Polish Opole and Silesian Voivodeships. Most of the Germans remaining in the territory following the end of the Second World War were expelled westward.

The earliest known reference to the town of Katscher dates back to 1321, although little is known about its early history until the period of the First Silesian War (1740–1742) between Prussia and Austria. Once the war had ended, most of Silesia, including Katscher, came under the rule of the Kingdom of Prussia. These events are closely connected to the emergence of the first Jewish community in the town. In 1787, just 36 Jews were registered as being resident there, but an independent Jewish community was not actually fully established until 1825 when the first synagogue was built. By 1840, the number of Jews living in the town had increased to 108. Five years later, a private Jewish school and a cemetery were established, and by 1871, the Jewish congregation or '*kehilla*' in Katscher had increased to 186. Around the beginning of the 20th century, some Jews left Katscher and moved to the bigger cities of Berlin and Breslau, which at that time had some of the largest Jewish populations in Germany. The 1910 census shows that only 52 Jews lived in Katscher, but following the plebiscite of 1921, many Silesian Jews decided to emigrate, although some actually opted to stay. In 1933, just 42 Jews were registered as living in the town (out of a total population of around 8,000), but by 1942, this number had been reduced to just 5 (Louis Böhm was one of the very last Jews to leave Katscher in 1943). As mentioned above, the anti-Jewish Race Laws which came into force in 1933 were not applied so strictly to those Jews living in Silesia, which meant that they managed to live in relative peace until 1937 when this protection was removed. Around this time, Jewish children were barred from schools in Katscher and were forced to attend the Jewish school in nearby Ratibor.

Pre-war Katscher showing former synagogue

A rather bizarre rule introduced as part of the Race Laws was that Jews were no longer permitted to visit barbers. This would have been a big blow to men in particular who used to go to the barber regularly to be shaved. In a letter written in June 1941, Louis complains about this new law.

'So, from today, I am forced to shave myself. I managed to survive the first attempt and hope that I can get used to it.'

During Kristallnacht in November 1938, the town's synagogue was burnt to the ground, and a small number of Jewish businesses and shops were also destroyed. It is highly probable that Louis Böhm's former shop that now belonged to Max Cohn was also targeted. The ruins of the synagogue were completely removed following the end of the Second World War, and the land was subsequently used to build houses on. The Jewish cemetery was also completely desecrated during the Hitler years, and the Polish authorities were then ordered to remove all human remains (see below). Today, there is no trace of the cemetery itself, but the location is marked by an area of green.

Katscher (Polish: Kietrz) today has a population of just over 6,000 inhabitants, and little remains of the picturesque town centre, which was burnt and completely destroyed by the advancing Soviet Army between January and March 1945 as part of the Upper Silesian Offensive.

Clearing the former Jewish cemetery in Katscher

This strategically significant Soviet military campaign sought to capture the substantial industrial and natural resources located in the region. Under the command of Marshal Ivan Konev, the 1st Ukrainian Front slowly pushed the Germans back towards the Czech border. In light of the significant importance of the region to the Germans, more and more troops were sent to defend the area, which slowed down the Soviet offensive considerably. It was not until the war had finally ended on 8 May 1945 that the Soviets could finally claim victory. But the cost in terms of human life had been extremely heavy. A total of 480,000 Soviet and German troops were involved in the Upper Silesian Offensive, and by the time the action was completed in the spring of 1945, more than 66,000 fatalities had been registered.

THE SIEGE OF BRESLAU

During the 1930s, Breslau had been home to several members of the Böhm family. Arthur, Clara and their two daughters moved there in 1930, and over the next few years, both Henry and Kate and George and Elfriede also lived there with their children. Fortunately, all of them, apart from Clara, were able to flee the city before the Second World War got underway. However, during the last two years of the war, Breslau became significant, as it was situated directly in the path of the advancing Soviet troops.

Prior to the Second World War, Breslau had been something of a model Nazi city where a staggering 200,000 people (51.7%) had voted for Hitler's NSDAP party in the 1933 elections. But following Hitler's rise to power, the Nazis tightened their grip on the city and launched a campaign of terror that eventually led to the murder of scores of Jews and other enemies of the state. Synagogues were burnt to the ground during Kristallnacht, and the guillotine in the infamous Kleczkowska prison saw plenty of action, with the decapitated bodies of political prisoners being donated to Breslau's medical schools. Yet in spite of the murders, persecution and strict rationing, the citizens of wartime Breslau generally fared better than their fellow Germans elsewhere in the German Reich did. Out of range of Allied air raids, Breslau's citizens were spared the nightmare of British carpet bombings, and the city came to be considered something of a safe haven, its population swelling to more than a million people as the conflict raged elsewhere.

However, by the second half of 1944, waves of German units had returned from the Eastern Front, exposing the lies behind Hitler's propaganda that had been reporting stories of great victories during the Russian campaign. Hitler subsequently declared that Breslau was to become a 'fortress' in light of the uncertain situation on the front and the expectation that, should the Soviets decide to advance westwards, the city of Breslau and Silesia as a whole would be very much in the front line. In fact, the so-called Vistula-Oder Offensive began on 12 January 1945, and it quickly became clear that it was only a question of time before the Red Army reached the city.

The decision to blockade Breslau would change the history and complexion of the city forever. With most of its civilian population now trapped within its boundaries, Breslau endured an epic 80-day siege that would cost tens of thousands of lives and leave the city a smouldering heap of ruins. The so-called Battle for Breslau ranks as one of the most savage sieges in modern history and was also among the most significant, if lesser-known, human tragedies of the Second World War. Truckloads of wounded people flooded the city's hospitals, and as the Red Army approached, the rumble of artillery could already be heard in the distance. Karl Hanke was appointed commander of the whole operation and set about the daunting task of turning Breslau into a fortress.

Two defensive rings were constructed around the city, with some fortifications located 20 kilometres outside the centre. Supplies were stockpiled and troops were mobilised. A garrison of some 80,000 men was hurriedly put together in what was planned to become the critical defensive element on the so-called Eastern Wall. In reality, however, these troops were a chaotic rabble consisting of Hitler Youth, First World War veterans, police officers, and tired and injured soldiers from retreating regiments. This mixed bag of men and boys was ludicrously ill-equipped to face the full force of the looming Soviet onslaught. As the countdown to the impending siege began, Hanke complained that he only had two tanks at his disposal, along with weapons that were either outdated or had been captured from previous campaigns in Poland, the Soviet Union and Yugoslavia. Despite that, he stubbornly refused to order an evacuation of civilians until 19 January 1945. But by this time, the majority of transport links had already been destroyed by Soviet shelling.

Thousands of people had been waiting anxiously to evacuate the city when they heard the news of the Soviet advance on 14 January 1945. But they were unable to leave for another six days because of damage to the railway tracks and almost continuous fierce fighting. In complete panic and desperation, between 50,000 and 60,000 people, mostly women and children, left on foot in exceptionally bitter winter conditions. This ended in tragedy when a short time later, 18,000 frozen bodies were recovered along the route, and it was also reported that 70 children had been crushed to death under the wheels of trucks. It is estimated that at least 90,000 citizens of Breslau died during this mass exodus from the city. But more than 200,000 people who realised that leaving on foot was madness remained in Breslau, and by February 15, the Soviet noose had tightened even further.

By now, the city was in a state of full-blown panic. Talk of defeatism was punished by death, and on January 28, Deputy Mayor Dr. Wolfgang Spielhagen was executed in the main square for this very reason. Execution squads roamed the city, murdering pessimists, looters and anyone found shirking their duty to the Fatherland. Finally, following a rapid advance, the Soviets encircled the city on 15 February 1945, and Breslau's fate was sealed. The Red Army launched a ferocious attack, deploying hundreds of tanks in the battle. But hopes of a quick Soviet victory proved to be optimistic, and the battle soon turned into a brutal massacre with both sides sustaining heavy casualties. In the first three days alone, the Soviets lost more than 70 tanks as the conflict descended into savage street fighting. Civilians and slave labour were deployed to help build fortifications, and vast stretches of the city were demolished so that bricks could be used to strengthen the defences. In a growing sign of desperation, even the university library was stripped of thousands of books, all destined for the barricades. In March, the residential area between the Szczytnicki and Grunwaldzki bridges was levelled to build an improvised airstrip that would, in theory, be Breslau's connection to the outside world. But this enormous project proved to be a complete disaster. With rations only issued to those who were still working and civilians being forced to work under fierce fire, more than 13,000 died when the Soviets bombed the area.

But worse was yet to come when, on 1 April, the Soviets launched a new offensive, and a particularly heavy bombardment saw much of the city engulfed in flames. The Nazi HQ was forced to relocate from the bunker on Partisan Hill to the university library, while fighting continued to rage in the sewers and houses on the fringes of the city. Even when the end was in sight, the Nazis fought bitterly to the last man, crushing an ill-fated uprising staged by those civilians who had chosen to remain in the city. Breslau finally capitulated on 6 May, and the peace deal was signed. The day before, Karl Hanke, the very man who had ordered the execution of anyone caught fleeing, took off from Breslau's makeshift runway in a plane reserved specifically for his escape. Having been appointed by Hitler to replace Himmler as Reichsführer-SS on 29 April, Hanke flew to Prague but was later captured by Czech soldiers and died on 8 June during an attempt to escape. Breslau was the last major city in eastern Germany to fall, doing so on 7 May 1945.

Although Breslau was only bombed once, massive destruction took place in the aftermath of the attack, and this once beautiful city was all but destroyed. The medieval parts and almost all of the historical landmarks were completely gutted. Those buildings that escaped bomb damage were subsequently burned and looted by the Soviets. Witness testimonies from the time report that a murdered, disfigured or disembowelled German could be found hanging from virtually every lamp post in the city.

For the remaining civilian survivors, the end of the war unleashed a new enemy. It is estimated that approximately two million German women were raped by Red Army soldiers on their advance westwards, and Breslau proved to be no exception as marauding packs of drunken troops sought to celebrate their victory. With all hospitals destroyed, and the main waterworks a pile of ruins, epidemics raged unchecked as the city descended further into a hellish chaos. Official figures state that in total, the Battle for Breslau had cost the lives of 170,000 civilians, 6,000 German troops, and 7,000 Soviet troops. More than 70 per cent of the city lay in total ruin (this can be partly attributed to Nazi efforts to fortify the city), 10 kilometres of sewers had been blown up and nearly 70 per cent of the electricity supply had been cut off. Of the 30,000 registered buildings in the city, 21,600 had sustained damage, with an estimated 18 million cubic metres of smashed rubble covering the entire area. The removal of this war debris lasted until the 1960s.

Under the terms of the Yalta Agreement, the new rulers of the city that would, from then on, be known as Wrocław arrived three days after the peace deal had been signed. Poles from the east flocked to repopulate Wrocław, lured by false rumours of jobs, wealth and undamaged townhouses. More than 10 per cent of these new settlers came from the eastern city of Lwów, and this mass migration was to irrevocably change Wrocław's demographic makeup. Black market trading and anarchy reigned as armed gangs of Russians, Germans and Poles roamed the streets at night, drinking, looting and shooting. It is believed that fortunes were made from theft and profiteering.

Reduced to slaves by their new masters, Germans were forced to make public apologies for their "collective guilt" at social and governmental gatherings. Others were sent to camps where conditions were unbearable. Of 8,064 Germans to be imprisoned in the notorious Camp Lamsdorf in Upper Silesia, 6,488 people, including hundreds of children, died from starvation, disease, hard labour and physical maltreatment that was also said to have involved torture. In addition, thousands died of sickness brought on by bad water, starvation and exposure, whereas many others committed suicide. The end of the war saw the start of an active campaign to 'de-Germanise' the city. Newspapers launched competitions as an incentive to completely eradicate all traces of Wrocław's German heritage with monuments, gravestones, shop signs and street signs all falling victim to this iconoclastic fury.

However, by the end of 1945, as many as 300,000 Germans remained in the city, many of whom had been temporarily relocated from Poznań, creating a pressing concern for the Polish authorities. Forced transports began in July, and by January 1948, Wrocław was officially declared to be free of all German inhabitants.

Viktoriastrasse, Breslau 1945 where George and Elfriede Böhm had lived

The so-called Sovietisation of the city soon followed, and Wrocław was chosen to host the Exhibition of Recovered Territories, which was in reality nothing more than a propaganda stunt designed to highlight the glories of Polish socialism. Attracting more than 1.5 million visitors during its three-month run, the exhibition finally closed at the end of October 1948, and with that, investment and national interest in Wrocław essentially died. For the next few years the city was to become nothing more than a feeder for Warsaw, with priceless works of art being transported to the capital. The main priority of the Polish government during this period was to rebuild its capital city as soon as possible, and in 1949 alone, approximately 200,000 bricks were sent daily to Warsaw to aid the reconstruction of the Polish capital.

THE FALL OF KATSCHER AND GLEIWITZ

Early in March 1945, the Soviet 4th Tank Army moved southward and launched an attack on German lines. This offensive effectively marked the end of so-called Operation Gemse. The troops broke through German lines west of Oppeln (now Opole, Poland) and advanced on Neustadt (now Prudnik, Poland) and Neisse (now Nysa, Poland), while to the southeast, other Soviet divisions attacked German troops and attempted to completely encircle them. A number of German units trapped at Oppeln were completely wiped out, and both Ratibor and Katscher were finally captured by the Soviets on 31 March. Marshall Konev announced the successful conclusion of the Silesia campaign, claiming that more than 40,000 German troops had been killed and 14,000 taken prisoner.

Having completely destroyed the town centre of Katscher, the Soviets also set fire to a number of buildings and completely terrorized the local population before continuing their push towards Berlin. Many towns were effectively left in ruins, and following the end of the Second World War, those Germans still living in the area were literally given 24 hours' notice to leave their homes and ordered to deposit their house keys with the authorities and to take only essential belongings with them.

When the new immigrants arrived after being driven out of their homes in those parts of eastern Poland which had now been handed over to Russia, they were simply told to choose one of the houses that had been left standing and collect the keys from the town hall. So literally within days, the entire German population of the town was simply replaced by Poles. Having stood empty for some time, Louis and Jenni's former home in Thrömerstrasse was finally acquired by the Szwej family who still live in the house today. The grandfather of this family had often talked about the invading Soviet troops and the time the family had first moved into Louis and Jenni's house.

'Grandfather told me that Katscher was badly bombed and the centre of the town was completely destroyed, but some of the outlying streets were spared. But there was a large bomb crater in the garden of the house which was derelict and in very poor condition. When we entered the house, we found a dead horse in the 'salon' (living room) which we assumed had run into the house to escape the bombing. There was also a dead cow in the basement which we think had also died after being frightened by the bombing.

At the front of the house there were a lot of spruces growing and bushes all in bloom. To the left of the house, there was a little garden with cherry trees and at the back of the house a beautiful gazebo. There were also nut trees and a small plot to the side where potatoes had been grown. Although people had told us that a Hungarian family had lived in the house, my grandmother always suspected that the previous inhabitants were Jewish because, in the salon, there was a kind of curtained-off alcove which my grandmother thought might have been used as a sort of prayer/worship area. When the Russians came through, they trashed the house, and we were shocked to see that they had even used this alcove in the living room as a toilet and had rubbed excrement all over the carpet and the walls. This is why we call the Russians "pigs". The kitchen was *in the basement, and there was a small lift which brought the food up to the dining room.'*

On the eve of the Second World War, the beautiful city of Gleiwitz and former home to George, Elfriede and their children Henry and Edith fell into disrepute following an event that was to have wide-reaching ramifications. The so-called Gleiwitz Incident was a covert Nazi German attack on the city's German radio station on 31 August 1939. The attack was a false flag operation, staged alongside two dozen similar German plots on the eve of Germany's invasion of Poland, with the attackers posing as Polish nationals. The Gleiwitz incident is the most widely known action of Operation Himmler, a series of special operations undertaken by the Schutzstaffel (SS) to serve Nazi German propaganda during the first days of the war. These operations were intended to create the appearance of Polish aggression against Germany in order to justify the invasion of Poland.

In 1945, at the Nüremberg War Trials, a German SS officer, Alfred Naujocks, provided evidence that revealed the truth behind what actually had happened in Gleiwitz. In his testimony, he admitted that he had organised the attack under orders from Reinhard Heydrich and Heinrich Müller, chief of the Gestapo. A small group of German operatives dressed in Polish uniforms and led by Naujocks himself was ordered to seize the Gleiwitz radio station and broadcast a short anti-German message in Polish. The aim of the whole operation was to make the attack and the broadcast look like the work of Polish anti-German saboteurs.

To make the attack look even more convincing, the Gestapo murdered Franciszek Honiok, a 43-year-old unmarried German farmer who was a known Polish sympathiser. The Gestapo had arrested him the previous day, dressed him up to look like a saboteur and then killed him by lethal injection and shot him to make his death look more authentic. Honiok was left dead at the scene so that he appeared to have been killed during the incident. His corpse was then presented to the police and press as proof of the attack. In addition, several prisoners from the Dachau concentration camp were drugged, shot dead and then had their faces disfigured to make identification impossible before their bodies were dumped at the radio station. In an oral testimony given at Nüremberg, Erwin von Lahousen stated that his division was one of two that were given the task of providing Polish Army uniforms, equipment and identification cards.

At the end of the war, Soviet troops swept through Silesia as part of their advance on Berlin, and on 23 January 1945, they seized Gleiwitz, as it had always been one of the major industrial centres in Upper Silesia. The Germans counter-attacked on the following day, precipitating a three-day battle for the area, but the city finally fell on 26 January. Over the next two days, a massacre of local inhabitants ensued, and Soviet soldiers set dozens of houses on fire, shooting those who tried to extinguish the flames. It has been estimated that the Soviets killed at least a thousand civilians in the area, many of whom were ethnic Poles and Silesians. As many as 800 of these deaths occurred as part of the Gleiwitz massacre. Following the killings, the victims were buried in a mass grave in a local cemetery. But during the years of communist rule in Poland, which lasted until 1989, knowledge of these events was strictly censored by the communist government, and the location of the mass grave was kept a secret. It was not until the 60th anniversary of the massacre in 2005 that a memorial stone was finally erected at the site of the cemetery.

A LAND TRANSFORMED

In those parts of Germany that had been handed over to Poland in 1945, more ethnic cleansing was to take place on an enormous scale. Those Germans who had not been expelled or had refused to leave faced severe reprisals or were even murdered. Catastrophic Allied bombing of Silesia during the Soviet advance towards Berlin in the spring of 1945 was followed by a huge wave of invading Soviet forces. The few surviving Germans in this region were hauled before Communist-led 'verification committees' which would decide their ultimate fate. The use of the German language and any civil rights that Silesian Germans had previously enjoyed were immediately suspended. Thousands of people died trying to flee, and more than a thousand slave labour camps were established in the eastern part of the Soviet Union. It has been estimated that about 165,000 Germans were deported from the German territories annexed by Poland and used as slave labour in the Soviet Union.

Following the defeat of Germany in 1945, the whole of Silesia was suddenly occupied by the Soviet Red Army, which embarked upon a horrendous spree of rapes and killings. In one instance, 182 Catholic nuns were raped in Neisse, and in the diocese of Kattowitz, the army left behind 66 pregnant nuns. Not even small children were spared the horrors of violent sexual assault, and little girls were sometimes attacked as often as their mothers. Boys who tried to protect their mothers and sisters were shot, as were many of the victims afterwards. It was actually Churchill who proposed the genocidal plan that was later adopted at the 1945 Potsdam Conference to 'put Poland on wheels and roll it westward' into German lands. As a result of this catastrophic solution to the so-called German Problem, millions of Poles were displaced from territories granted to the USSR, and many more millions of Germans were expelled from lands that they had inhabited since the 13th century.

Silesian Germans who, before World War II, had numbered around four million, were now collectively branded 'German partisans' and either fled, were murdered, put in camps, sent to the Gulags or expelled. Often, the men would be rounded up from the villages and camps and marched a short distance away to be shot and buried in mass graves. Under the terms of the agreements signed at the Yalta Conference of 1944 and the Potsdam Agreement in 1945, the whole region of German Silesia east of the rivers Oder and Neisse was to be transferred to Poland, and thousands of Poles from those territories farther east seized by Stalin were quickly trucked in and resettled there before the blood had even dried. Many Germans were even ordered to leave the beds made up with clean linen and to leave their house keys in the door when they surrendered their homes. This was an unbelievably cruel, yet efficient and well-planned operation.

But not all Germans were expelled, because some skilled workers and engineers were forced to stay, as the smooth running of industry depended on these people. In the Oppeln coal-mining region in Upper Silesia, some German miners and their families were allowed to stay, but their culture was repressed, and they were made to feel like slaves. Speaking German would be strictly forbidden for the next 40 years. The so-called Oder-Neisse Line became the new eastern border of post-war Germany.

The story of Upper Silesia since 1945 is complicated and is laced with apparent contradictions and ironies. Although the Soviets were intent on driving out all Germans from the region following the end of the Second World War and to completely eradicate every last trace of German life and traditions, the Soviets also realised that the factories had to continue to function and that it would therefore not be wise to intentionally deprive the area of valuable skills and expertise. As a result, thousands of skilled workers and engineers who could speak both German and Polish were forced to stay, take up Polish citizenship and renounce their German heritage and identity. These people were needed to keep the many coal mines and factories running during the critical postwar era. Those who refused to comply were forced to wear an armband with a large letter 'N', signifying that they were '*Niemiecki*' (German) and many were sent to Soviet labour camps in the East. From 1945 onwards, no one who did not hold a Polish passport was even allowed to own a house or flat. It was forbidden to teach German in schools or even to speak it in the home or in public, and across the whole region, an army of workers was deployed to laboriously remove German lettering from gravestones, memorials, shopfronts and public buildings. The name of every single village and town throughout Upper Silesia was changed to a Polish one, meaning that thousands of road signs had to be replaced. This was all part of the so-called *Entdeutschung* (de-Germanisation) process that continued for many years following the war's end.

However, many of the Germans who chose or were forced to stay were determined to resist this process and to retain as much of their German identity and heritage as possible, although this could only be done covertly of course. Many continued to speak German at home, thus ensuring that their children could be raised as bilingual, and they made every attempt to keep traditional German customs alive, particularly those pertaining to Christmas, religious traditions and typical Silesian cuisine such as *Streuselkuchen* (crumble cake) or *Sauerteigsuppe* (sourdough soup), which are still popular in the region today.

But animosity between the native Germans and the Poles continued for many years. German children were bullied at school and were often humiliated in public, and whole communities were discriminated against as part of an ongoing ethnic hate campaign. Although this situation improved somewhat as time passed, a real sea change did not come about until the fall of the Berlin Wall in 1989, which finally marked the end of the Soviet stranglehold and influence over Poland. Those Germans who had remained in Upper Silesia after 1945 were now free to express their 'Germanness' in any way that they wished, and the German language was once again allowed to be taught in schools. It is estimated that there are currently more than 200,000 people with German roots living in Upper Silesia, and there has been a renewed interest in and enthusiasm for the long-neglected treasures of German literature, music, art and history.

The beginnings of this new era for Upper Silesia saw the emergence of a widespread sense of pride in being Silesian, which has manifested itself in many different ways. Those people, both German and Polish, who were still able to speak Silesian, a dialect variant with Czech, Polish and German influences, delighted once again in being able to express themselves in their own unique way, and there are now around 60,000 native speakers of Silesian. Yet this new sense of Silesian national pride is not exclusive to the native Germans who live in the area. Many Poles too have become fiercely defensive of this unique part of western Poland. This is particularly noticeable in the main cities of Wrocław (Breslau), Opole (Oppeln) and Gliwice (Gleiwitz). In 1990, the Silesian Autonomy Movement was founded and, today, is led by Jerzy Gorzelik who has publicly claimed on many occasions that he does not regard himself as Polish but as 'Upper Silesian'. Since 1989, most road signs have displayed both the German and Polish names for towns, but Jerzy Gorzelik's movement, which is rapidly gaining momentum, is demanding, among other things, that all road signs be printed in Silesian, and he is also demanding more money for this wealthy part of modern-day Poland.

'We are officially the second richest of 16 voivodships in Poland, after Warsaw and Masovia, and provide 14% of the GDP,' says Gorzelik, 'and we feel we don't get enough back from the national government.'

The movement's slogan last year was 'Silesian Money for Silesian People'.

Today, Upper Silesia boasts a booming car manufacturing industry. Opel has a plant in Gliwice, and Fiat cars are produced in Tychy and Bielsko-Biala. Large chemical works operate in Kedzierzyn Kozle and Zdzieszowice, and the region has an enviable track record in scientific research, particularly in clean coal technology, soil detoxification and renewable energy. And the absolute jewel in the Silesian crown is undoubtedly the beautiful city of Breslau.

Breslau (Wrocław), the capital city of Silesia, was voted European Capital of Culture in 2016 and has undergone a radical transformation in the years since its massive destruction in the final months of the Second World War. Since its revival in recent years, this elegant cosmopolitan city is now being celebrated worldwide as something of a cultural magnet. With its 12 islands and 120 bridges, the city on the River Odra (Oder) is often dubbed the 'Venice of Poland'. Just minutes away from the imposing Gothic town hall that dominates its medieval market square stands the 695-foot Sky Tower, Poland's tallest skyscraper, which was completed in 2012 and is representative of a city that is a young, dynamic, high-tech hub. Today, this vibrant city of 640,000 people boasts literally hundreds of technology start-ups and alternative theatres. Breslau's 11 public and 22 private colleges produce 25,000 graduates each year. The city's universities, especially those focused on mathematics and physics, have helped Breslau successfully manage the transition from communism, and they have remained one of the city's major assets as much of Europe struggled with the debt crisis.

I am sure that if Arthur, George or Kate Böhm were alive today, they would almost certainly not recognise the completely reborn cities of Breslau and Gleiwitz. But I believe they would be heartened to see how their homeland Silesia has survived and completely transformed itself. When the thousands of new settlers arrived in this region from the East in 1945, they were newcomers without roots, and although those Germans who chose to remain there had lived there for generations, they too were newcomers in the sense that they had to become used to living in a completely new land with a new language and new traditions.

Market Square Breslau

It took more than 50 years for these two diverse peoples to learn to live together harmoniously. But today it is clear that integration has been largely successful and that the unique culture and traditions of Upper Silesia will continue to flourish for many generations to come. So just as the Böhms had managed to survive the horrific events of the Holocaust and rebuild their families in a new country, their former homeland, Upper Silesia, also emerged from virtual destruction at the end of the war to experience a truly remarkable rebirth.

PART III

RETURN TO THE HOMELAND

KATSCHER'S DARK HISTORY

My first visit to Katscher in the autumn of 1996 with my second wife, Judy, was an emotional yet fascinating experience. After a long, tortuous drive from the hotel where we were staying in Krakow, we finally arrived in Katscher just after lunchtime. We quickly found our way to the centre of this small, sleepy town, parked the car and stepped out into the crisp autumn sunlight.

We found ourselves standing in what had obviously been the town's main square but that bore very little resemblance to the old picture postcard I had brought with me. The photograph, taken in the 1920s, shows a picturesque marketplace bordered with pretty half-timbered houses and shops and, in the very centre, an ornate statue of what appears to be two figures standing on a raised column, each holding aloft a halo which bears a striking resemblance to a chimney sweep's brush. This statue was Katscher's imaginative depiction of the *Visitation of Maria*. But in 1996, the centre of the town was nothing more than a grassy recreation area with some trees and a few benches, one of which was occupied by three elderly men. Two of them were smoking pipes, while the other one seemed to be doing most of the chatting.

Market square, Katscher, c. 1925

We walked past the old men, along a pathway bordered by large shrubs, and there in front of us stood the statue from the photograph. Apart from a thick layer of black grime and a few chips, the monument was identical to the one in the photograph, so we knew that we must be in the right place. We stood and looked around us, but there didn't seem to be a single original building remaining from the time the Böhms had lived in the town. It now looked just like any other nondescript Eastern European town. With only one other photograph showing the street and the house on Thrömerstrasse where my great-grandfather Louis Böhm had lived, the difficulty of our task suddenly dawned on us. As there were very few people to be seen, we decided to begin our quest by speaking to the elderly men on the bench.

Apart from a few basic phrases, I had no real knowledge of Polish but knew that most of the older people living in that region would probably still understand and be able to speak some German. However, I also knew that the Germans were still hated by many Poles, so as we approached the group of pensioners, I was certainly not expecting to receive a friendly reception. I greeted the men in a friendly fashion in German, explaining that I was English and that my mother's family had lived in the town before the war. I showed them the photograph of the house and asked whether they knew whether it still existed. The pensioners looked at the ground and then at each other before mumbling a few phrases to each other in

Polish. Then the tall thin man in the middle addressed me rather curtly in broken German: 'We can't help you. Go and talk to the fat lady in the clothing shop over there.' He made a vague gesture towards the far corner of the square, looked away and engaged himself once again with his friends.

We walked into the shop the old man had pointed out to us, not really knowing whether he had just been trying to get rid of us. It was scantily stocked with ladies underwear, rolls of material, sewing accessories and balls of knitting wool. One or two people were browsing, but there was no sign of anyone behind the counter. After a few moments, a large lady in a red, tent-like floral dress emerged from a doorway at the back of the shop. I went over to her, smiled and after uttering a few pleasantries, asked her the same question I had put to the old pensioners. Her German didn't seem to be much better than that of the old man. But she managed to tell me we should just wait there, as she needed to fetch someone else who would be of more help to us. She waddled over to the doorway behind the counter and shouted what was probably a person's name into a gloomy corridor that led away from the back of the shop. After a few moments, a young boy of about ten appeared and looked at the buxom lady enquiringly. She spoke to him quickly, pointing to us at the same time and then gesturing out the window. As the boy made his way across the shop towards us, the lady motioned to us that we should follow him, as he was going to take us somewhere else. I was beginning to feel that maybe we had inadvertently stumbled into a Kafka novel and started to doubt that we would ever find out anything of value at all.

The boy walked out of the shop quickly, not even bothering to check if we were behind him. We rushed after him as he disappeared up a narrow alley which led away from the main square. For about ten minutes, he led us through alleyway after alleyway past some very ramshackle houses, along a walled pathway, past a beautiful church which I recognised from an old tourist guide of the area my aunt Ilse in Sydney had given to me eight years before, and finally came to a halt in front of what seemed to be the presbytery attached to the Catholic church. He led us into the large porch of the house, gesturing that we should sit on the wooden bench in front of a huge oak door. For a brief moment, he looked intently at the row of doorbells, each with a small nameplate under it. Then he pressed one of the buttons and promptly disappeared.

After a short pause, the door was opened by a tall, grey-haired priest who smiled at us benevolently, greeted us in Polish and ushered us into the hallway. He showed us into a small narrow office, closed the door behind us, beckoned to us both to take a seat and settled himself into a leather chair behind a desk which had a large engraved Bible on it. I asked whether he could speak German and was pleased to hear him answer in the affirmative, speaking German perfectly with just a trace of an accent. For the third time that day, I told the story of my mother, her family and their life in Katscher, showed him the old picture from the 1930s and asked him whether he could provide us with any useful information.

Father Tomasecki smiled broadly as it became clear that I had just asked him a question about one of his favourite subjects. He told us that he was the ideal person to help us because he was in fact the local historian and had taken a great personal interest in the German history of Katscher (Kietrz) and the subsequent development of the town into what was now a small, yet obviously close-knit, Polish community.

He then gave us a very vivid and detailed account of the events that had occurred at the end of Second World War when the Germans had retreated after wreaking havoc on the local communities. But he said that these events were tame compared with the atrocities that were yet to be committed by the advancing Soviet troops who swept through Silesia shortly afterwards during their final push towards Berlin. The widespread brutality, rapes, killings and devastation committed by the victorious Red Army have been well documented and certainly partly explain why most Poles today hate the Russians with a vengeance.

Father Tomasecki gazed thoughtfully at my black-and-white postcard of the town square, shook his head and explained that the Soviets had completely torched the centre of the town during their advance westwards towards Berlin. This, he said, explained why only the religious monument had remained, still blackened by the fire and smoke which had enveloped the idyllic birthplace of my mother. He handed the postcard back to me and picked up the second photo showing what, prior to 1945, had been Thrömerstrasse, with the former home of Louis and Jenni Böhm situated halfway along the street. His eyes lit up as if he had just recognised a long-lost friend. 'I am delighted to tell you that this house still exists today,' he said with a very satisfied smile. He took a small piece of paper and quickly drew us a sketch of how to get to the former Böhm residence on the outskirts of the town. With that he shook my hand, wished us good luck and showed us the door.

As we walked through the pretty garden of the presbytery back towards the town centre, I felt elated, as it was now clear that our long journey had not been in vain. The former home of my great-grandparents was still standing and was now just a short walk away. How I wished that my mother could have been there with us to share this momentous experience. Like many refugees, she had always insisted that she would never return to Germany after having been driven out in 1939, just eight months before the start of the war. However, in 1976, just a year before her death, I was teaching English at a school in Trier, West Germany, as part of my university studies. I managed to persuade her that she should come to see for herself how successfully Germany had developed into the leading European powerhouse and what a huge difference the so-called '*Wirtschaftswunder*' (Economic Miracle) had made to the lives of ordinary Germans.

But observing my mother in Germany and among Germans again was not an altogether comfortable experience for me. My brothers and I had always teased her for having forgotten most of her German and not having learnt much English. As we sat around the dinner table on a mild May evening in 1976 with the Blum family, with whom I was lodging at the time, it quickly became clear that my mother had indeed forgotten much of her German. Although she obviously understood everything, her own spoken German was faltering and clumsy. Moreover, I could see from her body language that she no longer really felt at home with Germans and was finding it difficult to relate to them. She later confided in me that these 'modern-day' Germans as she called them had reminded her very much of Americans, as they boasted about their big houses, big cars, large pensions and grand ambitions to once again live in a united Germany with a proud capital city, which would of course be the absolute jewel in the crown. At the time, my mother was highly critical and deeply sceptical of such talk, but the irony is that, in 1989, just 12 years after her death, such aspirations were about to become a reality as the Berlin Wall fell. Today, the magnificent city of Berlin is again the seat of the German government and stands proud at the very heart of a now-united Germany.

Ruth Böhm (r.h. side) with Fritz and Hilde Blum, Trier 1976

Father Tomasecki's hastily scribbled map proved to be surprisingly accurate as we wandered back across the square, down a narrow street at the far side and around a corner to finally enter what was clearly the street we had been searching for. As we stood at the end of the road and gazed into the distance towards what is now the border with the Czech Republic, we felt like excited archaeologists entering a sacred tomb for the first time since it had been closed off to the world centuries earlier. We looked at the photograph of the street which had been taken sometime around 1936 and were surprised to see how little had changed over the past decades. Virtually all the houses in the photograph were still standing, and many, if not most, had not been altered significantly during the intervening years. We walked slowly down the street and stopped dead in our tracks to face the house that, three-quarters of a century before, had been the home of Louis and Jenni Böhm.

The house looked much more modest than I had expected, and even though I had studied the photograph on many occasions before our visit, I was somehow expecting to see something grander. Set on quite a large plot of land with mature trees on either side, it had a grey concrete exterior, steep gabled front, a red tiled roof and a large bay window which was also tiled and seemed to incorporate some kind of porch to one side. Two tall chimneys emerged from the roof, each held in place with a supporting metal brace about halfway up. The two main windows facing the street were very distinctive, each having a curved lintel and enclosing three vertical panes of glass.

Standing in front of this house, looking at the old photograph, we were astonished to see that the neat railings and double gates at the front had not changed at all. Nor had any significant improvements or changes been made to the exterior of the building during the previous 60 years.

It was clear that there was a very large garden at the back of the house which did indeed look as expansive as my mother had described it. It really was not difficult for me to picture those large family gatherings during the summer which my mother had so often told me about.

Louis and Jenni Böhm's house in 1996

We deliberated for some time whether we should knock on the door and ask the owner if we could look around. However, we eventually decided that this was probably not a good idea because, by the time of our visit in 1996, it had become possible for Germans to reclaim property taken from their parents and grandparents at the end of the Second World War, although this had not been the case with Louis and Jenni's house. As a result of this decision by the German courts, there was an even higher degree of animosity and suspicion towards German visitors than there had been previously. I had no desire to upset the present residents of my great-grandparent's former home. It was enough for me that I had been able to make the trip, see the house with my own eyes and managed to correctly place yet another piece of the puzzle.

Although Katscher was essentially a rural town surrounded by farmland and lush meadows, there was in fact a fair amount of industry there, mainly weaving, rug-making and cloth processing. The town had a long history of weaving dating back to the mid-1800s. Apparently, the Troja, which flows through Katscher, used to change colour almost daily as dye from the weaving factories and workshops flowed into the river. However, the largest of these factories came into disrepute after the war when it was rumoured that large quantities of human hair shaved from the heads of prisoners in nearby Auschwitz were being used in the production of cloth. These rumours have persisted for the last 75 years.

On the basis of these rumours, new details have recently been uncovered about the so-called Poland Camps, one of which was located in Katscher. These camps were established at the beginning of the Second World War in Silesia to hold those Poles classified as 'unreliable' by German officials. In the aftermath of World War I, many of these people had wanted Silesia to become part of Poland and were branded anti-fascists because they had refused to allow themselves to be inscribed in the 'German folk list' to avow their 'Germanness'. Most of the Poland camps were located near the southern border of what had been Upper Silesia. The conditions in these camps were reported to be exceptionally hard and usually involved forced labour.

In February 1943, 20-year-old Halina Stanko was brought to the Katscher 'Poland 92' camp which had been established inside the town's carpet factory. She later told a news magazine how, together with dozens of other prisoners, and under armed escort of German guards, they were brought to the factory grounds every morning. She remembers that there had been a special entrance to the rug and yarn production area. 'At the time, we heard that they were using human hair', she says. There were also other people in Katscher who remember that human hair was being used in the Schaeffler factory. A woman living in the vicinity of the factory recounted that after the war, her father-in-law had become a director of the firm and in 1946 had found bales of human hair in the main warehouse. This would appear to correspond with the report provided by the former technical director of the Schaeffler textile factory, Heinrich Linkwitz, who, in May 1946, testified before a prosecutor in Gliwice that in 1943 two railway cars, loaded with human hair, had arrived in Katscher, each with a payload of 1.5 tons. The hair was processed into yarn at Schaeffler's, but apparently it had not been possible to process the entire stock by the time the war finished.

The former Schaeffler factory in Katscher

During my second visit to Katscher in September 2018, I was told by a local historian who had lived in the town for many years that these rumours were in fact true. As recently as April 2018, an article appeared on the Spiegel TV Polish website claiming that the old factory, the ruins of which still exist today, routinely employed Polish slave labour and did indeed regularly receive bales of human hair from Auschwitz to use in its production. The deputy head of the Auschwitz Museum's research department, Dr Jacek Lachendro, told Spiegel TV that part (1.95 tons) of the hair still exhibited in Auschwitz today was found in the factory in Katscher at the end of World War II. He also said that there were transcripts from the interrogation of former factory workers claiming that, in 1943, two train wagon-loads of hair were delivered to the factory. Tests conducted later by Polish authorities confirmed that it was indeed human hair and that it contained traces of Zyklon B, the same poison used in the gas chambers in Auschwitz.

Today, Schaeffler AG is one of Germany's largest automotive component suppliers, employing around 92,500 people in 50 countries. Although on the Schaeffler AG's website, the company's official history only begins in 1946, its sinister early years in Katscher and the company's association with and support of the NSDAP seem to be indisputable facts. In spite of numerous articles about the company's wartime activities that have been published since 2009, Schaeffler has always denied that it was involved in any kind of forced labour or that human hair was used for the production of fabric at its factory in Katscher.

So the pretty little market town of Katscher nestling peacefully among the gently undulating meadows of the Silesian countryside was where the story of the Böhm family had begun sometime around 1885 when Louis and Jenni Böhm decided to put down roots in the town, set up a business and start a family. And over the next four decades, the family flourished and, by all accounts, led a largely peaceful and happy life until the rise of Hitler in 1933. Up until that time, all the members of the small Jewish community in Katscher had been allowed to live their lives freely and in harmony and were well integrated into the local community. However, by the spring of 1945, all but five of the remaining Jews had been driven out of Katscher, a large part of the town had been burnt to the ground, the Jewish cemetery had been desecrated and the sinister activities of the Schaeffler Company had cast a dark stain over the history of Katscher. And the vestiges of these events still remain today.

I do not believe that either my mother or any other members of the Böhm family who survived the war had any idea about the shocking events that took place in their hometown following the end of the Second World War. As Lucy and I walked around Katscher (Kietrz) in the autumn of 2018, reflecting on the fact that this drab little Polish town no longer bore any resemblance to the charming, thriving community that it once had been when the Böhms were living there, I felt a great sense of sadness at what had become of my mother's hometown. Within a few hundred metres of the house where this decent, middle-class Jewish family had lived before the Second World War stood the ugly remains of the factory where slave labour had been employed and hair shaved from the heads of Jewish men, women and children was used to manufacture clothing to support the Nazi war machine. Ironically, this was the very factory that had supplied Louis with fabric during the years that his shop was still in business. Just around the corner from the Schaeffler factory lies an area of lush grass which marks the place where the Jewish cemetery used to be before all the graves were dug up and emptied and the gravestones completely destroyed. One of these graves would undoubtedly have belonged to my great-grandmother Jenni Böhm who died in March 1941. The tragedy of this sequence of events representing as it does the complete obliteration of all traces of Jewish life in Katscher is something that will always remain with me.

RETRACING THE STEPS

Breslau Main Station (today, Wrocław Główny Station) is a very imposing building that dates back to the middle of the 19th century. With its impressive castellated facade, vaulted Gothic arches and extensive interior wood panelling, it is not difficult to imagine what a hub of activity this place must have been during the pre-war years when so many thousands of people were desperately trying to leave the city.

Breslau central railway station

Although the interior of the building has been partially modernised, the original style, ornate arches and features have been carefully retained and given a new lease of life. In September 2018, as my daughter Lucy and I stood near the old-fashioned ticket office silently observing the steady stream of people coming and going, I found myself thinking about my mother and what must have been going through her mind as she passed by this very spot in May 1939 on her way to a new life in England and what she hoped would be freedom.

However, standing in front of the Odertor Railway Station (today, Wroclaw Nadodrze Station) situated in a northern suburb of Breslau was a completely different experience. We both felt the same sense of dread and tragedy, feelings no doubt evoked in part by the depressing redbrick facade which had clearly not changed for decades and also by the knowledge of the terrible events that had taken place here between 1941 and 1942. Although, at the time of our visit, the station was still in use, it had apparently been earmarked for demolition, which probably explained why the whole building looked so run-down and almost deserted. The main vestibule was shabby, unlit, damp and smelly and was virtually empty apart from a few people shuffling their way to the platforms.

We soon found proof of the sinister history of this notorious place in the form of a bronze plaque on one of the walls, a memorial to the more than 7,000 Jews who were deported from this railway station in the space of just 18 months. My maternal grandmother, Clara Böhm, was one of the 7,000. We walked up to one of the platforms and stood there for a few moments staring along the tracks, trying to imagine the panic and sheer human despair and misery that must have been present as the dozens of cattle trucks were crammed full with terrified men, women and children to be transported to their deaths.

Odertor Railway Station

The *Hala Targowa* (Market Hall) has been a regular feature of everyday life in Breslau since the beginning of the 20th century. Built between 1906 and 1908, it is an imposing building that houses Breslau's largest food market which somehow survived the bombing of 1945 virtually unscathed, although it was extensively modernised in 1983.

There can be little doubt that those members of the Böhm family who had lived in Breslau during the 1930s regularly shopped here, as its huge selection of fresh fruit, vegetables, meat, fish, spices, herbs and flowers would have been unsurpassed elsewhere in the city. And this is still the case today. Before the Second World War, two main public synagogues existed in Breslau – the so-called New Synagogue which was destroyed during Kristallnacht in November 1938 and the White Stork Synagogue (see below) which, although heavily damaged, actually survived the pogroms.

Breslau Food Market

There were also numerous private synagogues, all of which were destroyed. Although the precise dates are somewhat vague, it is clear from family letters that various members of the Böhm family together with their spouses and children lived in Breslau during the 1930s. George and Elfriede Böhm and their children Henry and Edith were resident in the city for a while, as was George's brother, Arthur, his wife, Clara, and their two children Ruth and Ilse. Kate, Henry Schweiger and their children Gary and Steffi also lived there for some time after being forced to leave Katscher sometime around 1935. It is not clear how religious the Böhm family members were, but I believe it is highly likely that they must have been familiar with both of the major synagogues in Breslau.

During our visit to Breslau in 2018, Lucy and I spent a memorable morning looking around the White Stork Synagogue, which is situated just a short walk away from the city's huge market square, known as the Rynek (Polish: market). The synagogue, which opened in 1829, is a three-story neoclassical building that architect Carl Ferdinand Langhans designed. The original interior, now lost, was designed by the painter Raphael Biow, whereas the name was taken from an inn of the same name which had previously stood on the site. The main prayer hall is surrounded on three sides by women's galleries, and two levels of galleries to the north and two on the south flank a single gallery on the eastern Torah ark wall. The wooden frame of the Torah ark and the damaged tablets of the

Ten Commandments are all that remain of the original religious features. During Kristallnacht, the interior of the building was destroyed by the *Sturmabteilung* who also tore up the scrolls. On the same night, the New Synagogue, which served the city's liberal community, was burned to the ground by Nazi paramilitary groups.

White Stork Synagogue, Breslau

White Stork Synagogue, Breslau

The White Stork synagogue, which at the time served mainly Conservative Jews, escaped that fate because it was located close to other buildings, and the perpetrators of the pogrom were concerned that a fire might spread to non-Jewish structures.

As has been previously stated, in 1930 Arthur Böhm, his wife, Clara, and their two daughters left their grand house in Katscher and moved into an apartment in Kronprinzenstrasse, Breslau. There is virtually no mention in the surviving family documents that sheds any light on what life was like for the family living in the city in the 1930s. However, it is possible to make an educated guess at this because other residents of the city did actually record the worsening daily situation of the 20,000 or so Jews who were listed as still being resident in Breslau in 1933. As mentioned in the prologue, one of the most detailed of these accounts is *No Justice in Germany – The Breslau Diaries 1933–1941* written by Willy Cohn (1888–1941) who was regarded as one of the most important writers of his generation.

Cohn paints a vivid yet disturbing picture of how, after Hitler had come to power and the harsh Nuremberg Race Laws had been introduced in September 1933, life gradually became increasingly difficult (and in some cases unbearable) for Jews living under the new regime. Jewish judges, university professors, teachers and scores of other public employees were sacked, Jewish businesses and shops were boycotted and Jews of all ages were subjected to verbal and physical abuse on a daily basis. There was strict food rationing, and in 1935, all public swimming pools were closed to Jews. This would undoubtedly have been a blow to my mother who had always been a keen swimmer.

After 1937, as the Nazis' grip on Germany tightened even more and as war began to look inevitable, more and more draconian laws were introduced, the main objective of which was to completely exclude Jewish people from everyday society and to effectively prevent them from earning a living or preserving their wealth. Public humiliation became a central element in marginalizing the Jews. As we already know, barbers were forbidden to shave Jews, and public libraries were off limits to Jewish people. Once war had broken out, Jews were no longer even allowed to own radios.

Following the Order for the Disclosure of Assets which became law in April 1938, Jews were required to report all assets and property in excess of 5,000 Reichsmarks. Hitler visited Breslau on at least two occasions. In March 1936, he attended a mass NSDAP rally in the city which drew crowds of thousands, and in September of that same year, he was in the city again to open the new Breslau-Kreisbau section of the autobahn as part of his ambitious plan to dramatically improve the road and rail infrastructure throughout Germany. The real reason however behind this huge investment in infrastructure was that Hitler was preparing for war and wanted to ensure that troops, armaments and supplies could be moved around the country quickly.

Along with Berlin and Frankfurt, Breslau had been one of the major centres of Jewish life in Germany in the pre-war era. There is no doubt that life for the many thousands of Jews living in these cities had become more and more difficult as war approached. Once Hitler had come to power, those Jews with the foresight and means quickly realised that their only hope of survival would be emigration, although this was by no means a straightforward process even at this early stage. But after Kristallnacht in November 1938, it gradually became even more difficult to obtain a visa, as the numbers of Jews trying to leave the country had soared and the number of countries willing to accept them diminished. And by early 1940, it had become almost impossible to leave, so those Jews remaining in Germany had little choice but to prepare themselves for their inevitable fate.

Grüssau Monastery (today Krzeszów, Poland) is situated about a two-hour drive west of Breslau. This impressive monastery in Lower Silesia was founded by Anna of Bohemia in 1242 but was later largely destroyed during the Thirty Years War. From 1728 onwards, it was restored in the ornate Baroque style. After being secularised during the Napoleonic War, it was again raised to a monastery by Pope Pius XI in 1924, but in 1940, the Nazi government seized the monastery and converted it into a transit/detention camp for Jewish prisoners.

Grüssau Monastery

The NSDAP and the regional government of Lower Silesia established the camp in Grüssau for those Jews of the district who had been evicted from their homes by the Nazi authorities. This place of temporary internment prior to the Jews' deportation to extermination camps in the East and to the Theresienstadt ghetto was housed in this Cistercian monastery and was officially designated as a 'Housing Commune' (*Wohngemeinschaft*). Although very little is known about the camp, it is estimated that a total of 960 Jews were detained in Grüssau, beginning with the first transports on 10 October and 13 October 1941. Apparently, physical conditions were very harsh, and heating was sporadic, if not non-existent. Starting in 1942, the prisoners of Grüssau were deported to the Theresienstadt ghetto and to the German extermination camps in Poland. The camp was finally liquidated in 1943. In an entry in his diaries from 16 October 1941, Willy Cohn writes:

'Grandmother Proskauer came yesterday afternoon, she wept. Up to now we have received only unwelcome news from Grüssau. Among other things, the beds hadn't arrived yet, and people had to sleep fully clothed.'

Sometime around the middle of November 1941, my maternal grandmother Clara Böhm was arrested in Breslau and transported from the Odertor railway station to Grüssau Monastery. In one of her letters written in March 1942, Clara reveals that at least two of her relatives were also being held in Grüssau at the same time.

'Aunt Johanna is also here, and she is very worried about me. She comes to see me quite a lot. Uncle Wiener is here as well, which is great comfort to me.'

My mother had often said that she could not understand why Clara had made a special point of mentioning relatives in this letter whom she had not seen or talked about for years. As part of the mass roundup of Jews that took place across this region following the Wannsee Conference, it was usual that, having arrested one member of a family, the Gestapo would also do everything they could to detain all other remaining relatives. This explains why it was usual for whole families to be deported to the extermination camps together. She remained in the camp until April 1942 when, it is believed, she was sent to Theresienstadt, where, just one month later, she died. The numerous letters Clara wrote to Ruth during her time in Grüssau also contain one or two remarks that are rather puzzling.

She describes her surroundings as being pleasant and comfortable and even talks of receiving visits from some of her friends from Breslau. This description in no way fits with contemporary accounts of everyday life in the camp where a completely different picture emerges, that of a harsh, unheated and strict prison where food shortages and sickness were common. I think that it is highly unlikely that prisoners were freely allowed to receive visitors. In fact, there is no reason to suppose that life in Grüssau was any less harsh than in any other camp such as Dachau, Theresienstadt or Buchenwald.

It remains something of a mystery therefore as to why Clara chose to describe her time in Grüssau as something resembling a stay in a comfortable country hotel. I believe that the most likely explanation is that she did not want to alarm her daughter by revealing the real truth about her time in the monastery and why she was there in the first place. Or maybe, being the naïve person she was, she simply had not grasped the real reason she had been sent there. In fact, my mother had often confided in Peter, my eldest brother, that she could never understand why her mother's last letters had been sent from a monastery. It may be the case that Ruth never knew the real truth about what Grüssau was used for between 1941 and 1943. Even today, this sinister period in the monastery's history is covered up or simply glossed over wherever possible. During our guided tour of the buildings and the grounds, I asked our guide on two separate occasions about the period during which the monastery had been requisitioned by the Nazis, but my question was met with a wall of silence.

The thrilling highlight of our trip to Upper Silesia in 2018 was beyond doubt a visit to Louis and Jenni's former home in Thrömerstrasse, Katscher. All of their six children, Arthur, George, Kate, Rudi, Walter and Siegbert, were registered as being born in Katscher between 1885 and 1898, so I believe that Jenni and Louis probably lived in the house from the late 1800s until Louis finally left in 1943.

Three generations of the Szwej family have now lived in the house since 1945, and thanks to the universal reach of social media and some good luck, I managed to make contact with Kasia, the granddaughter of the person who had acquired the house after the war. Over a period of six months or so preceding our visit, we exchanged lengthy emails which not only provided me with a wealth of anecdotal detail about the house itself but also made it possible for Kasia and her family to at last discover something about the family that had lived there before them. They had long suspected that the house had been inhabited by a Jewish family but had been unable to find out any concrete information. My mother had always described the house as a 'villa', a word which is rather suggestive of a rather grand house in its own grounds. It was indeed set on its own expansive grounds which surrounded the house on all sides, but from the front at least, it did not appear to be overly spacious. The roof, detailing around the windows, external woodwork and the garden railings and gate looked exactly the same as on the old photo of the house from around 1930 that we had found among my mother's documents after she had died.

So on a crisp September morning in 2018, my daughter Lucy and I stood outside what used to be No 3, Thrömerstrasse feeling excited yet somewhat apprehensive as we contemplated the huge significance of being the first family members to set foot inside the former home of Louis and Jenni Böhm for 77 years.

Louis & Jenni's house c. 1930

Kasia and her family were all very welcoming and had even drafted in an interpreter for the day, as their knowledge of English and German was limited. We were treated to a delicious lunch of wholesome Polish food, cakes, coffee and wine, and as we sat around the table in the spacious sitting room where my great-grandfather had hosted so many happy family functions, the conversation flowed freely as detail after detail about the history of the house and the town gradually emerged.

It was clear that all the internal woodwork and features on the ground floor of the house had been carefully retained and lovingly restored by Kasia's family. The glass-panelled wooden doors, high ceilings and ornate cornices really gave us the feeling we were stepping back in time. However, the upper floors of the house had been completely remodelled and converted into a self-contained apartment. But the main reception/dining room on the ground floor had obviously not changed substantially since the 1930s.

The rooms in the basement are now used mainly as a storage area, but when Louis and Jenni lived in the house, their loyal maidservant/cook, Anna Jaschke, had her living quarters there, next to the kitchen.

With the Szwej family, September 2018

An interesting detail that emerged during lunch was that there was actually a lift, a so-called 'dumb waiter' that was used to transport food from the kitchen up to the dining room. Anna worked for the family for more than 25 years and, we believe, remained with Louis right up until the time he was transported to Theresienstadt.

Drawing room, Thrömerstrasse

At the back of the house is a large garden now used mainly as a storage area, as many of the original trees and shrubs have long disappeared. There used to be an ornate gazebo in the garden which Jenni and Louis made extensive use of for special functions whenever the whole family got together and which is shown in the photo taken during the 1920s. Kasia told me that her family had removed the gazebo many years earlier because it had fallen into disrepair, but they have since replaced it with a more modern one.

As we all gathered in the garden near the spot where the gazebo used to stand to say our final goodbyes to the Swezj family at the end of our incredible day in Katscher, Kasia suddenly hugged me and started sobbing uncontrollably. After a few moments she managed to calm herself and, in her broken English, told me how deeply the story of the Böhms had affected her and how special it was to have met Louis and Jenni's great-grandson and great-great-granddaughter. At the time of writing, we are still in regular contact, and we both feel there is a close bond between us and that we will always remain friends.

With Lucy outside the Böhm house

Our final destination during our Poland adventure was the Auschwitz and Birkenau concentration camps. '*Arbeit macht frei*' ('Work is liberating') proclaims the ornate slogan over the main entrance gates to the Auschwitz I camp.

Auschwitz I, main gate

This slogan contains three short words, 15 letters and two spaces meticulously crafted out of fine metalwork and interlaced into a delicate filigree as if it were some kind of fancy lace banner. Yet this simple phrase represents one of the biggest deceptions of modern times. For the 400,000 people who, between 1940 and 1945, walked under that sign into the camp, neither work nor anything else would ever free them from a wretched existence of misery, torture and starvation that, for most, would end in death.

As we walked through those gates on a chilly September day in 2018, we could not help but feel a sense of guilt, for we knew that in only a few hours, we could simply stroll back out of the camp again to freedom. The countless books, films, personal accounts and narratives written about Auschwitz completely fail to prepare one for the harrowing, numbing experience of walking in complete silence shoulder to shoulder with weeping strangers through the chilling, dimly lit corridors, cells and crematoria of this dreadfully tragic place.

My maternal grandmother Clara Böhm, my great-grandfather Louis and my great-uncle Siegbert were just three of the six million Jews who were murdered during the Holocaust. Trying to identify with this many victims is an impossible task. Mass slaughter on this scale simply defies human comprehension but on the day of our visit to Auschwitz, I felt that somehow I had to identify with the victims because in a sense I am a survivor. As a Jew, I am a member of a people that was almost completely extinguished by the time Hitler made his token gesture to mankind by shooting himself through the head in a bunker in Berlin in 1945.

An old university friend once told me something I have never forgotten. He said that he believed that, when we are faced with something too huge to comprehend, we should focus on the detail because the detail forms part of the whole and, like human genes, this detail can reveal valuable information about the bigger picture. This is exactly what I resolved to do during our visit to Auschwitz. Neither of us could even attempt to understand the attempted annihilation of a complete ethnic group, but we were determined to study the exhibits on display inside the orderly red blocks of the Auschwitz I camp and attempt to reconstruct the whole picture of the indescribable human tragedy that had unfolded there.

When the Soviets liberated the Auschwitz-Birkenau camps on 27 January 1945, they found 43,000 pairs of shoes waiting to be shipped to Germany to help those (non-Jewish) civilians who had lost everything during the relentless Allied bombardment of their cities. These shoes now fill one half of an entire barrack room. This is one of the most pitiful sights I have ever witnessed. At first, this small mountain appears to be just a heap of decaying rubbish. But as Lucy and I moved closer to the glass screen and peered into the gloom beyond, we could see black leather shoes, brown shoes, pink shoes, blue shoes, strapless shoes, slippers, shoes with buckles, shoes with straps, shoes with heels missing, brown boots caked in mud and brightly coloured shoes which looked as if they had belonged to young village girls in love with their land and in love with life. And there were the children's shoes – from tiny little bootees for a one-year-old taking her first cautious steps and sensible black walking shoes for energetic five- and six-year-old toddlers to more stylish red slip-ons for those bubbly teenagers on the brink of womanhood.

We drifted on slowly in a kind of trance through rooms crammed to the ceiling with artificial legs, arms and crutches, past a display cabinet containing 6,000 assorted hairbrushes, clothes brushes, toothbrushes, shaving brushes and combs. I stood in speechless horror before a mountain of suitcases and bags belonging to 10,000 dead people, each daubed with a crudely painted name. When we got to the final room in Block 5, which a sign proclaims is dedicated solely to the 'Material Evidence of Crime', we noticed quite a large crowd in front of an enormous glass-fronted display cabinet which occupied almost the entire length of the room. Most were standing in silence, but some were sobbing quietly. We moved forward to get a glimpse of what it was they were looking at.

When the Soviets revealed to the world a crime the scale of which was unprecedented in human history on that icy winter's day in January 1945, perhaps their most gruesome discovery was a warehouse full of sacks of human hair which had been shaven off the heads of at least 140,000 people. This sickening testament to the systematic murder of millions of innocent men, women and children now fills an entire room in Block 5 of Auschwitz 1 camp. The cabinet is lit only dimly so that the hair does not degrade any further under the glare and heat of electric lights. But as we braced ourselves and moved closer to the glass to peer inside, we could clearly make out mounds of grey hair, black hair, blonde hair, red hair, brown hair, wispy hair, curly hair, straight hair, braided hair, coarse hair and fine hair, but perhaps most tragically of all, there was also a great deal of what was clearly children's hair, much of it still held together in bunches with the tattered remnants of coloured ribbons and bows.

We walked on in a kind of numbed silence past the entrance to the crematorium and the single gallows where the last Kommandant of Auschwitz, Rudolf Höss, was hanged in 1947. We looked across to the luxury villa which Höss had had constructed in such a way that he would be able to watch his victims entering the crematorium from the comfort of his bedroom and felt emotionally drained. But we knew that we were now about to embark on what would be the most difficult part of the whole trip, the visit to Birkenau some two miles away. Auschwitz 1 had originally been established merely as a concentration camp, although thousands of people were subsequently murdered there. But Birkenau (Auschwitz 2) had been designed and built solely as a killing factory.

Having got off the courtesy bus that had taken us from Auschwitz 1 camp to the Birkenau camp, we walked towards the main entrance arch following the railway line which the Germans had constructed when they built the camp in 1940. We looked along the length of the tracks as they passed under the single redbrick watchtower, through the gates and into the heart of the camp. As we cast our eyes along the length of the perimeter fence, it was clear that, unlike Auschwitz I, this camp was built on an enormous scale occupying the same area as a small town. We walked slowly along the railway tracks leaving the main entrance behind us, both feeling the same sense of desolation at being in this place. We made our way towards the so-called selection area and, beyond it, the 'shower rooms' and the crematoria.

The railway track continued in a completely straight line ahead of us for about five hundred metres through the gigantic selection area, which could accommodate 5,000 people, coming to an abrupt stop at two large buffers in the distance just before a line of trees. Running parallel with the railway line and bordering the selection area on both sides is a high, electrified fence which originally enclosed two separate camps – the women's camp to the right and the men's camp to the left. When it was fully operational, Birkenau could accommodate up to 150,000 inmates, although 75 per cent of the people who arrived on the numerous transports from Germany and beyond were sent straight to the gas chambers.

Only those who were fit enough to work or who could serve some other purpose were allowed to live for a while longer before also being sent to their deaths. As we continued walking along the railway line towards the buffers, all those graphic accounts of the Birkenau selection process which I had read suddenly came back to me with vivid clarity and realism. After having spent several days incarcerated inside stifling hot cattle trucks in horrible conditions, those people who had survived the journey were dragged out into the daylight and onto the dusty gravel of the selection area. They were ordered to line up with their belongings, and the lottery would begin. A unformed official, usually a doctor, would move along the line carrying a baton and carry out a scant visual examination of the members of this human cargo. Those deemed to be unfit or infirm were ordered to the left, whereas the people who looked as if they were capable of work were ordered to the right. So it was that, with a simple arm gesture, entire families were split up in the cruellest of ways. Hordes of sobbing people watched their loved ones being dragged off to their deaths knowing that they would be left to grieve and to suffer for only a short time before being forced to join them.

Auschwitz-Birkenau Camp

We stopped just short of the railway buffers and reflected on the fact that this had quite literally been the end of the line for the 1.3 million Jews, Romani, Poles and people with mental/physical disabilities who it is estimated, were murdered at Auschwitz-Birkenau between 1942 and 1945. We looked beyond the line of trees to the crumpled remains of the crematoria and gas chambers which the Germans had blown up just before the camp was liberated by the Soviets in a hurried attempt to conceal the evidence of their atrocious crimes. When the camp was fully operational, the four main crematoria were kept working continuously for three years, burning 1,200 bodies in each 24-hour period with an efficiency which, even today, simply defies the imagination.

Sitting in the hotel bar on our last evening in Breslau, Lucy and I reflected on the events of the preceding week as we tried to put into words, share and somehow make sense of some of the many emotions and impressions that were clearly occupying both our minds. Our emotional journey retracing the footsteps of the Böhm family had taken us from a sleepy little town in Upper Silesia where life for the family in the years between 1880 and 1930 had been idyllic and peaceful to Breslau, a stylish university city which had once been home to one of the largest Jewish populations in Germany.

In Breslau, we had visited the apartment building where George and Elfriede Böhm had lived after leaving Katscher, and we had stood in silence inside the city's two railways stations from where various members of the family had been forced to leave Germany. For some of the family, it was to be the start of a journey to freedom and a new life in a foreign country. But for others such as Clara Böhm, it was to be a final journey to meet their end in a Nazi camp.

From there, we travelled to Grüssau monastery where Clara and other Jewish deportees were held in dreadful conditions before being sent to their deaths in Theresienstadt and Auschwitz. And it was in the Auschwitz-Birkenau death factory that we concluded our visit. Our tour of the camp, depressing and harrowing though it was, did however compel us once again to reflect on the fate of the six million Jews who were murdered during the Holocaust as part of Hitler's master plan to create an Aryan super race.

During the flight back from Breslau, my thoughts turned once again to Louis and Jenni Böhm, their six children and the quiet, prosperous life and business they had built for themselves in a sleepy little town nestling amongst the rolling meadows of Upper Silesia.

I suddenly felt a wave of self-doubt about the huge project that lay before me. Would I really be able to achieve what I had set out to do – to tell a story that would follow the various members of the family and their individual destinies and to set my narrative against the political and social context that had had such an influence on every member of the family and had become interwoven with the life-changing events that each one of them was forced to live through?

During my research, I discovered many surprising facts about the Böhm family, and thanks to those surviving members of the family who generously provided me with photographs, letters, anecdotes, official documents and personal accounts, I believe that I have been able to form a picture in my own mind of what kind of people the Böhms really were. Louis and Jenni were born at a time when the traditional Prussian Jewish values of family, hard work, respecting the will of God and the community and increasing one's prosperity for the good of the family as a whole were all important. This was an honest, hard-working family who passionately believed in their country and were prepared to fight and, if necessary, die for it. Four of their sons fought in the First World War, and two of them, Arthur, my grandfather, and his brother George were even awarded the German Iron Cross. Yet when disaster struck and the comfortable life which the family had built for themselves started to disintegrate, the Böhms proved to be real survivors. Those members of the family who were able to leave Germany before the Hitler regime made everyday life for the Jews impossible showed great courage, determination, flexibility and a capacity to endure and overcome extreme hardship, personal loss and tragedy.

The Böhms were tough people who were not only capable of surviving periods of almost unimaginable misery and suffering but also were able to cling to hope and to rebuild and create new families, homes and businesses of their own. I believe that they all shared a love of nature and the countryside and enjoyed good food, laughter, stylish clothes, tasteful furniture, music and culture. Although they were much better off than many of their contemporaries, I do not believe that they were at all snobbish or arrogant. Louis was a highly respected member of the local community in Katscher. He was well liked and believed in treating everyone fairly, irrespective of background, social standing or creed. He was the undisputed head of the family and clearly greatly enjoyed the regular family gatherings he and Jenni hosted in their house and garden in Thrömerstrasse. I believe that theirs was a harmonious family, as there is no evidence in any of the remaining letters of any major dispute or conflict, although clearly there must have been the occasional disagreements that occur in most families.

A SURPRISING DISCOVERY

The research I had carried out prior to writing this book lasted for two years and revealed many new facts about the Böhm family, along with several surprises. But perhaps the biggest surprise of all was discovering who the real father of my eldest brother Peter was. While I was in the middle of researching my mother's background, I found myself heading off down something of a side alley because it had never been clear who Peter's father actually was. In Part One of the book, I suggested that the prime suspect had always been Fritz Pelikan who had come from the same area as my mother and whom she had known quite well before going to England in 1939. In fact, both the Pelikan and Böhm families were well acquainted with each other, and there was even a suggestion within the family that Ruth and Fritz had been unofficially engaged. My mother arrived in England in May 1939, and Fritz Pelikan followed in July of that year. Like many young Jewish male refugees, Fritz was sent to the Kitchener camp, near Sandwich in Kent, on his arrival in Great Britain, on his way to the United States. The Alien card he was given when he landed at Dover stated:

'Leave to land is hereby granted at Dover on condition that the holder proceeds forthwith to Richborough (Kitchener) Refugee Camp, registers at once with the police and remains at the camp until he emigrates.'

The Kitchener inmates enjoyed a high degree of freedom and were even allowed to leave the camp during the day and make trips within the local area. In his book *From Dachau to Dunkirk*, Fritz describes his time in the Kitchener camp in great detail. He was apparently befriended by a local lady, Joyce Piercy, and her sister who both took a keen interest in many of the young Jewish men arriving at the camp.

As has already been mentioned in Part One, Fritz was often invited to afternoon tea with the Piercy sisters and actually spent Christmas with them at their home in 1939. The Piercy sisters were also known to Clara Böhm, as she mentions them in one or two of her letters to Ruth. They may even have played a part in obtaining an exit visa for Clara to leave Germany, although, tragically, she was never able to make use of it. In early December 1939, Ruth gave up her job with the Sadler family in Abbots Langley and travelled down to Kent, presumably to meet up with Fritz. It may even be the case that she also spent Christmas with the Piercys. Early in 1940, Fritz Pelikan managed to join the Pioneer Corps, a branch of the British Army which recruited foreign nationals. Ruth became pregnant in February 1940, and one month later, Fritz left the United Kingdom for France. He survived the war, and after leaving the army in 1948, he moved to north London with his wife, Vera, where he set up a carpet shop which he owned until his death in 1993. After the war, he changed his name to Fred Pelican.

In her letters to her mother during this period, there is no hint of a doubt that Ruth wanted Clara to believe that Fritz was Peter's father – or she actually believed herself that Fritz was indeed the father. Also, a letter that Ruth received from Fritz's mother at the beginning of August 1941 makes it absolutely clear that Ruth must have told her mother and the Pelikans that Fritz was Peter's father:

'Daddy and I cried with joy over little Peter. I am glad that Fritz is

healthy and that he is pleased with little Peter. How I would love to have my first grandchild here with me.'

However, my mother had always told me that Peter's father had trained as a doctor and that he had died during the D-Day campaign in June 1944. She would also often show me a photograph of Peter's father. After reading Fritz Pelikan's book which contained several photos of him, I concluded that this could not have been the same man who Ruth had claimed was Peter's father. There was simply no physical resemblance to the person in the photos in the book. Also, Fritz Pelikan had no medical background whatsoever. So in the spring of 2018, I concluded that Peter's real father must have been someone else.

Emil Brand c. 1935

As part of my preparation for writing the book, I translated a large number of letters that were in my mother's possession when she died. One of these letters had been sent to her from New York in 1942 by a man called Emil Brand. My subsequent research into Emil Brand revealed that he was born in Vienna in 1912 where he attended medical school until May 1939 when he was forced to leave Austria because, following the Anschluss, everyday life for

Austrian Jews had become impossible. (The 'Anschluss' describes the annexation of Austria on 12 March 1938.)

He managed to get to England via Belgium and was immediately sent to the Kitchener camp. Since he had been living in Austria and my mother had lived in Germany, it is unlikely that they would have met before going to England. But it is clear that they did meet sometime between May 1939 and February 1940 when Peter was conceived. We can only speculate as to how the two of them initially got together, but the most likely theory is that they met through Emil's sister, Lilly, who, like my mother, had also managed to get a job as a domestic help with a family living in north London, not very far from Abbots Langley where my mother had been working for the Sadler family. Furthermore, the Lyons Corner House close to The Strand in London was a popular haunt for Jewish refugees both before and during the Second World War and would have been only a short train ride for my mother and Lilly Brand. Was Ruth Böhm first introduced to Emil by his sister at the Lyons Corner House sometime during the second half of 1939? We will never know for sure, but this theory seems to be the most plausible one. The other possibility is that because it is known that Emil Brand was also acquainted with the Piercy sisters, he could have met my mother through them. Another rather intriguing aspect to this mystery is that in a letter Ruth received from her mother on 6 June 1941, Clara reveals that Emil had actually been in contact with her:

'I was really astounded to get a letter from Emil Brand in New York. I have already sent him a reply. He could have written long ago. His letter was dated 29 April and took about four weeks to reach me.'

If Ruth and Emil had just enjoyed a brief fling together, it is difficult to understand why he would have gone to the trouble of writing to Clara, presumably to introduce himself. Furthermore, the phrase *'he could have written long ago'* in her letter would seem to suggest that Clara had been expecting Emil to make contact with her, which means that Ruth must have already spoken to her mother about her relationship with him. The tone of Clara's letter leads me to believe that the relationship between Emil and Ruth was probably more than just a fleeting wartime romance. Moreover, it is clear from his letter of 1942 that Emil knew that my mother had a child, but nothing in the tone of the letter suggests that he either knew or believed that he was the father, although he does not hold back from expressing his opinion as to how Ruth should bring up the child (see extract below). If Ruth knew at that stage that he was the real father, why she chose never to tell him will forever remain a mystery. Whatever her reasons, she always maintained that Peter's father had died in June 1944.

'It would be much, much better if you could get a factory job and put Peter in a nursery so that you can also have a life for yourself. If you have a live-in job, you have to be available 24 hours a day. It would be much better for Peter if he could grow up amongst other children and (in a nursery). He would at least be properly taken care of whilst you are at work. Don't take another domestic job which wouldn't be easy to get anyway if you have a child because then you would be very handicapped in the job.'

And that would have been the end of the story had I not discovered during the course of 2018 that Emil, who died in Florida in 2001, had a daughter who was still alive and living in New York State. Once again, thanks to the internet, various search engines and the invaluable Ancestry website, I was able to track down his daughter, Ellen Brand, and even managed to find an email address for her.

I subsequently forwarded everything I had found out about Emil and Ellen to my brother Peter in Sydney. Needless to say, it took him some time to process all of this new information before deciding what to do next, but after a couple of months, he plucked up the courage to write to Ellen Brand. Following a lengthy delay, Ellen finally responded, and although she had known almost nothing about her father's time in England or his connection with my mother, she and Peter agreed to do a DNA test to establish whether they were really related. The result was unequivocal. They were indeed half-sister and brother. So at the advanced age of 78, my brother had finally discovered who his real father was and, in the process, had also acquired a half-sister, not to mention an extended family in the United States.

Peter Vincent and Ellen Brand, July 2019

But for me, the absolute icing on the cake was a fascinating postscript to this story that occurred early in 2019. In 1996, as part of the Steven Spielberg Shoah Foundation Holocaust Survivor Stories programme, Emil Brand had recorded a one-hour video interview during which he talks at length about his early life in Vienna, his escape from Germany, his time in England and the new life he had built for himself and his family in the United States. The Brand family kindly made this video available to me.

Up until that point, Emil Brand had been nothing more than a name on the bottom of a letter or at the top of an official document. But now, for the first time, here was a real person, a sprightly and alert 84-year-old who sat opposite me, looked directly into the camera and simply talked about his fascinating life. It was a fantastic experience, and finding out about him and his daughter, Ellen, was undoubtedly one of the highlights of the whole research project.

The preceding account is my attempt to tell the story of three generations of the Böhms, a well-to-do Jewish family from Upper Silesia, over a period of almost 100 years, during which the life of every single member of the family was to change irrevocably. Admittedly, there have been thousands of Holocaust survivor stories written since the end of the Second World War. In addition, there are also countless documentaries, Hollywood films, face-to-face interviews and lengthy newspaper articles, all of which have tried to capture something of the despair, hopelessness, tragedy, resilience and sheer will to survive of those Jews who lived and died during the Holocaust. But this is the story of *my* family, and this fact does I believe make the above account all the more poignant and relevant.

As I have already mentioned, my personal objective in writing this book was to attempt to reconstruct as much of the story as possible through the lens of a member of the fourth generation of the family. I had known very little about my mother's family background until my mid-20s, by which time she was already approaching the end of her life. Over the 40 or so years which have elapsed since then, I have experienced many mixed emotions about my Jewish heritage, and there have certainly been times when I have struggled with my own sense of identity in light of my newly acquired knowledge about my mother's background.

However, today I can say that I have never been more proud of my German/Jewish background. It is my hope that this book will prove to be of lasting interest and value to both current and future generations of the Böhm family.

Compiling the family tree, researching individual members of the family and bringing their truly remarkable story to life has proven to be an immensely enriching journey for me, and although it has occupied me for close to three years, it has undoubtedly been one of the most fulfilling experiences of my whole life.

EPILOGUE

As I embark upon this, the concluding section of the book, the world finds itself in crisis on a number of different fronts. Firstly, we are currently in the middle of the COVID-19 pandemic, and it is an inescapable fact that this crippling sickness has already exerted a terrible human toll across more than 200 countries, having infected more than 75 million people, not to mention the catastrophic effects it has had worldwide on stock markets and business confidence, which will undoubtedly have dire consequences for many years to come. The number of lives lost and the sheer level of human suffering and economic and social disruption and damage that has resulted as a consequence of this global scourge is truly staggering.

Whole countries have found themselves in a 'lockdown' situation, and for many people, normal, everyday life has virtually come to a standstill. Millions of people all over the world have been confined to their homes like prisoners and can do nothing but watch helplessly as, one by one, the familiar cornerstones of their routine existence are chipped away. No one knows when or how this nightmare will end, but we can be sure that, for many of us at least, life will never be quite the same again.

Secondly, after hundreds of years of selfish abuse by a human race obsessed with its own self-importance and driven by rampant consumerism, our entire planet is now at risk. Flooding the atmosphere with toxic carbons, destroying the world's rainforests and robbing the earth of its valuable natural resources can only ever continue for so long. We are now perilously close to the tipping point, beyond which there can be no way back, no way of restoring nature's delicate balance and no way of returning the earth to its once beautiful and harmonious equilibrium. Add to this a worldwide population that is fast approaching ten billion, poverty and starvation throughout the underdeveloped countries and a completely uneven distribution of wealth meaning that more than 90 per cent of all the money in the entire world is firmly in the hands of less than 10 per cent of the population, and we are facing a global humanitarian crisis of truly apocalyptic proportions.

Thirdly, in large parts of the developed world, particularly the United States, Europe, South America and the Middle East, the political landscape has been completely turned on its head. It can justifiably be said that populism has replaced principles. Millions of citizens in many countries have completely lost confidence in their politicians, and the hitherto secure, moderate centre ground is now fast disappearing with millions of voters increasingly moving to the extreme right, intent on putting often dangerous personalities in power, rather than seasoned politicians. As a result, true democracy has been degraded, and several countries are now perilously close to becoming fascist states. Furthermore, antisemitism and other forms of religious and racial intolerance and persecution are yet again very much on the increase. It is estimated that approximately 70 million refugees have been displaced from their homes over the last seven years as a result of wars, religious persecution or poverty. These people are now desperate to build new lives elsewhere, yet many developed countries have cruelly decided to close their borders to anyone who is not 'one of their own'.

Ours is a very different world from the one that my great-grandfather Louis Böhm grew up in. By my estimation, there are currently around 80 surviving descendants of Louis and Jenni Böhm, all of whom are, to a certain extent, already feeling the effects of our rapidly changing world as described above. For many of us, life is not as comfortable as it was previously, and we can no longer be sure what the future holds for us. Yet I would venture that the fear and uncertainty which the fourth, fifth and sixth generations of the Böhm family feel is nothing compared with what our ancestors had to endure during the period of the Second World War and the Holocaust. Louis and Jenni were a devoted couple who, over a period of 40 years, raised a large family and built a thriving drapery business. They instilled in their children the well-trusted, traditional values of tolerance, fairness, belief in God, sense of community and humanity and were convinced that they had given their offspring a firm foundation on which to build happy and successful lives for themselves and their respective families.

I believe that if Louis and Jenni had been Catholic or Protestant, their hopes and aspirations for their children would have been fully realised. But they were Jewish, and once Hitler had come to power in 1933, the fate of this decent middle-class family from a small town in Upper Silesia was firmly sealed. As a result of the 1933 Race Laws, the simmering antisemitism which had existed in German society for generations suddenly burst to the surface and propelled the country into what would be one of the darkest chapters in human history. But I am convinced that, had they lived longer, Louis and Jenni would have been immensely proud of Arthur, George, Kate and Walter, the only four members of the second generation of the Böhm family who were lucky enough to survive the horrors of the Holocaust.

In spite of his many faults, Arthur had managed to get by for more than six years under what must have been very difficult circumstances in Manila during the Second World War. I believe that he was a streetwise individual with good instincts and a natural charm, which no doubt would have helped him considerably in making friends and persuading people to do favours for him. He had always loved money, fine clothes, good food and wine, nature, travel, adventure and, above all, women. There can be little doubt that he was something of a womaniser, as there are numerous family anecdotes which would seem to support this. According to Kate, as Clara was giving birth to her first daughter, Ilse, upstairs, Arthur was busy seducing one of the maids downstairs. Years later, after his arrival in Sydney, he was living with a certain Mrs Pengelly in Sydney who was actually his landlady. However, on one occasion when his grandson Ronny Hirsch paid him a visit, Arthur was seated in an armchair with Mrs Pengelly nestled on his lap, her arms entwined amorously around his neck. It is a bizarre coincidence yet factually true that, before this lady immigrated to Australia, she had lived in South Wales and, for a short time, was actually one of my father's girlfriends. Perhaps Arthur could best be described as a 'lovable rogue' who, I am sure, never realised his full potential in life. Having reviewed everything I know about him, I am left with the lasting impression that, following the excitement of fighting for the Fatherland during the Great War and being awarded the Iron Cross, everything that followed proved to be something of an anti-climax. He was rather vain, was always immaculately dressed, had a high opinion of himself and fancied himself an astute businessman, which he most certainly was not. He seemed to be most interested in achieving the 'good life' by investing the least possible effort. But he was passionate about nature, was also interested in farming and adored travel and adventure.

Although he failed to be offered any meaningful jobs after arriving in Sydney in 1946 and seemed to be always plagued by financial difficulties, I believe that he did find some form of peace and fulfilment in his later years prior to his death in 1970.

Arthur Böhm

Sadly, as a result of the permanent rift with his youngest daughter, Ruth, in 1954, he never got to know the five grandchildren he had in the United Kingdom (my side of the family). In spite of having two additional grandchildren in Sydney (Ronny and Tamar) and an extended family that included his brother, sister and various nephews and nieces, I believe that he led a largely solitary existence during his final years. For some time, he lived on Bribie Island, just off the Queensland coast where I understand he had a kind of smallholding, complete with chickens and pigs. When he was in Manila, he also had a pet pig whom he called 'Nuchie' and was apparently very attached to. He would have been very happy on Bribie Island, I am sure. His final months were spent in a care home in very poor health, but even here, Arthur refused to abandon the habits of a lifetime and never gave up trying to seduce the nurses. At the time of writing, there are 29 direct descendants of Arthur Böhm. His two daughters, Ilse and Ruth, have left him five surviving grandchildren, 12 great-grandchildren and 12 great great-grandchildren.

Kate had been the first of the Böhms to feel the full force of the wave of hate and resentment unleashed on German Jews in Upper Silesia following the plebiscite of 1921. She and her husband, Henry, were forced to simply stand by and watch as a torrent of anti-Jewish feeling swept away their livelihood, destroying their hopes, their belief in humanity and ultimately any chance that they might have had of leading a normal life. We cannot imagine what it must have been like to watch the successful business they had worked so hard to build burnt to the ground by people who used to be just good neighbours but had suddenly become their enemies. But Kate and Henry were made of strong stuff, and undeterred, they moved to another area, set up another business and simply carried on with their lives.

In spite of the further tragedy that Kate was to endure in 1955 when, in the space of six short months, she lost both her husband and daughter, she once again found the necessary strength and will to carry on. But 13 years later, in 1968, Kate suffered yet another blow when her son, Gary, died of cancer. At this stage, many people within the family thought that this event would mark the beginning of the end for her, but just six weeks later, she had resumed her favourite hobby of playing cards and, once again, had managed to pick herself up and continue living. After selling her house to developers in 1965, Kate bought herself a flat in Randwick where she lived until 1980, when she was persuaded to move into the Montefiore Home in the Hunters Hill area of Sydney where she spent the rest of her life.

In 1963, at the age of 69, she even passed her driving test, bought herself a Morris Mini and, by all accounts became an absolute terror on the roads, yet, miraculously, was never fined for her many misdemeanours. In addition to her passion for card playing, she also loved spending time at the local B'nai B'rith lodge.

Today there are 24 surviving descendants of Kate Böhm and Henry Schweiger. Their daughter, Steffi, and her husband, Walter Freeman, had two children, Susan and Stephen, who still live in

Sydney and have played their part in helping expand the fifth generation of the Böhm family by producing four children and four grandchildren between them. Steffi's brother, Gary, and his wife, Joyce Watson, had three children, Katryn, Michael and David who, collectively, have produced five children and eight grandchildren. Katryn lives in the Grampians area of Victoria with her partner, Ron, whereas one of her brothers, Michael, lives in the United States.

Kate Böhm 100th birthday

Kate Böhm lived through the Holocaust, was branded a pariah by her fellow Germans, was systematically driven out of her home and country and saw members of her family die in the death camps. It is beyond my comprehension how Kate found the will to carry on living, particularly after her tragic losses in 1955 and again in 1968. But carry on living she did, even managing to celebrate her 100th birthday in style in 1995 before her death later that same year.

Kate Böhm was a truly exceptional woman who stubbornly refused to let life get the better of her, and as Louis and Jenni's only daughter, she proved herself time and again to be the undisputed matriarch of the family, embodying as she did the very best qualities her parents had instilled in her. I would like to pay tribute to this truly remarkable woman.

George Böhm

Like his sister, George Böhm was also made of strong stuff and proved over and over again that he too could successfully build a new life for himself in a different country. With a thriving dental laboratory in Sydney and his family close around him, George settled very well into his new life in Sydney after arriving from Shanghai after the war. He was even lucky enough to find love again in his second wife, Fanny Epstein, who had arrived in Australia in December 1938, having sailed from Bremen. Today there are 26 surviving descendants of George Böhm.

His son, Henry, and his wife, Lilly, are survived by their four daughters, all of whom still live in Australia. The four Böhm girls have made a prolific contribution to the expansion of the family, having collectively produced 11 children and 11 grandchildren. So over a period of just 13 years starting in 1885, Louis and Jenni Böhm, despite living through what was undoubtedly one of the darkest and most tragic chapters in human history, succeeded in creating the beginnings of a dynasty that would span the world and is still thriving 160 years later. Today the many descendants of Louis and Jenni Böhm are spread across Australia, the United Kingdom, Israel and the United States.

Böhm/Vincent family reunion, Sydney 1986

This decent, unassuming middle-class couple from rural Upper Silesia ran a thriving drapery business for the whole of their working lives, and there is no doubt that shop-keeping was very much in the Böhm blood, as this tradition continued over the years through various branches of the family. George's son, Henry, and his wife, Lily, also ran a successful haberdashery and clothing business for many years, as did Ilse's daughter, Tamar, and her husband, Werner. Kate and Henry set up and ran several shoe shops during their life, a tradition inherited by their son, Gary, who established a retail business in Cooma, New South Wales, initially involved in supplying protective footwear to people working on the Snowy Mountain Hydro-Electric project. Ilse's son, Ronny Hirsch, was for many years CEO of the WC Penfold Group which, at one time, was Australia's largest stationery chain.

But many of the Böhm descendants have also achieved success in a wide variety of other professions that have no connection with retailing. These include law, mental health, business, accountancy, local government, sales, human resources, hospitality, fashion, tourism, teaching, transport and logistics, librarianship and the arts and entertainment. Gary Schweiger had always been a keen skier, and with great enthusiasm, he shared his passion for this sport with his children. His daughter, Katryn, actually qualified to compete in the 1964 Winter Olympics, but sadly her professional skiing career later came to an abrupt end as a result of a serious car accident. Katryn's brother, Michael, graduated from the National Institute of Dramatic Arts alongside Mel Gibson and now runs a successful entertainment company from his home in Long Island. One of Henry Böhm's daughters, Jenni, worked for several years as a make-up artist for the ABC television company and later retrained as an art therapist. As a young man, Arthur Böhm played the violin and was also a keen dancer, and Clara was an accomplished pianist, so a love of music and a talent for dancing is something they passed on to their daughters, particularly to Ruth, my mother. My younger brother Ken is a talented guitarist, and I have enjoyed a passionate love affair with the piano and all kinds of music that has lasted 50 years, and even now, a day hardly goes by when I do not sit at the keyboard and play something by Bach, Mozart or Gershwin. My eldest brother, Peter, inherited my mother's ballroom dancing talent and, as a young officer in the merchant navy, could often be spotted in the middle of the Atlantic or Pacific Ocean giving dancing lessons to a motley crew of swarthy deckhands aboard one of BP's oil tankers. Ilse's daughter, Tamar, is an accomplished sculptress and painter.

Ruth's favourite cousin, Henry, and his wife, Lilly, enjoyed a long happy marriage that was to last for an incredible 57 years before Henry finally died in 2015. His daughters remember him as a kind, gentle, fun-loving man whose main priority was always to simply provide for his family.

He was apparently very generous with his time and had a special gift for treating everyone he met in such a way that they would immediately feel like an old friend. He would often speak with great fondness about his early life in Katscher and those wonderful occasions in which he was able to spend time with his grandparents and cousins.

Yet in spite of the tragedy heaped on his family during the Holocaust and his own terrible ordeal aboard the Dunera, Henry never expressed any bitterness about any of these events or about the destruction of his homeland during the Third Reich. He considered himself a wealthy man, but not in monetary terms, and loved nothing more than relaxing in the garden, reading a newspaper and simply enjoying the quiet harmony of family life. His eldest daughter, Susan, describes him as a real 'mensch' (man of worth).

Henry Böhm, Lilly and family 2003

After finding each other in 1957, Ilse and Walter subsequently spent 47 happy years together before Ilse's death in 2004. Although she frequently enjoyed a flutter on the poker machines and became very proficient at completing German crossword puzzles, she and Walter also shared many common interests. They loved animals, had several pets and became members of Sydney's Taronga Zoo, which they used to visit regularly. Apparently she was a doting grandmother and, like her sister, Ruth, was also very good at baking cakes and enjoyed creating many delicious recipes including yeast cakes and nut cakes topped with chocolate icing.

Walter loved classical music, was also an avid book collector and did a lot of volunteer work, including visiting members of his synagogue who were ill in hospital. During the years I lived in Sydney, I got to know both Ilse and Walter very well.

My lasting impression of my aunt is that of a warm, slightly reserved yet spiritual woman who, in spite of having to endure periods of extreme hardship and emotional turmoil during her life, always seemed to manage to find the silver lining and simply carry on. I am sure that her parents and grandparents would have been justifiably proud of her.

Ilse and Walter Freeman

Ultimately, the fact that so many members of the fourth, fifth, and now sixth generations of the Böhm family have been so successful in their lives does I think reveal something about the values and characteristics we have all inherited from Louis and Jenni. These include a desire to serve and be of value to other people, perseverance, imagination, intelligence, tolerance, openness, a love of life and a sense of adventure. I am convinced that these qualities will continue to prevail in successive generations of the family and will prove to be the true legacy of Louis and Jenni. In a sense, we are all a continuation of their story. Yet none of us should allow ourselves to forget the extreme hardship and tragedy that our forefathers had to endure to enable us all to be alive in the world today enjoying the freedom, high quality of life and limitless choice that we undoubtedly have.

Writing this book has been not only a process but also a journey, one that has taken me back in time to another era and into another world to attempt to reconstruct a story that no one who is alive today could possibly have told. To do this, I have spent many long months searching every possible source for the tiniest snippets of information that could enable me to correctly place another piece of the puzzle. I have translated dozens of family letters and read each one repeatedly searching for any clues that might be hidden between the faded lines of writing. I have studied almost 100 photographs, often with the aid of a magnifying glass, painstakingly trying to identify yet another person or place that could help bring this story to life.

The Böhm Descendants. Kate Schweiger's 100th Birthday Celebration, Sydney 1995

I have searched virtually every online database and archive and copied and recorded hundreds of documents, many of which have provided me with additional valuable details about the Böhm family and their life in Katscher. I have walked the same streets in Breslau, Ratibor and Katscher that my forefathers would have walked along almost a hundred years ago, and I have sat in the elegant sitting room of Louis and Jenni's house in Thrömerstrasse and felt their presence like never before.

I have walked through the corridors of the school in Katscher which the Böhm children would have attended and have stood silently on a long-abandoned piece of ground that marks the spot where my great-grandmother Jenni Böhm was laid to rest in March 1941. I have stood on the platform at the Odertor railway station in

Breslau, from where, following her arrest, my maternal grandmother, Clara Böhm, was herded into a cattle truck to be transported to a concentration camp.

In Grüssau monastery, I sat quietly on a chair in the very building where she was imprisoned before being sent westwards to the Theresienstadt ghetto where, we believe, she finally met her end. I have walked along the railway track inside the Auschwitz-Birkenau concentration camp and felt the deepest sense of despair and utter incomprehension as I stood in front of the ruined crematorium where my great-uncle Siegbert was gassed in 1942.

But this book has also taken me on another, more intimate journey, deep into my own psyche. Writing the story of the Böhm family has forced me to look again at who I really am, to re-evaluate my life and values and perhaps to finally make sense of the unease, confusion and depression I have often felt at various stages of my life.

Many Jewish people of my generation see themselves as survivors of the Holocaust, although they were not alive at the time and clearly did not experience any of the terrible events their ancestors had to endure. Personally, I do not subscribe to this belief, nor do I see myself as a Holocaust survivor, in the strictest sense of the word, for the reasons stated above. But at the same time, it would be naïve and simply wrong to say that the Holocaust and the experiences my mother, grandparents and great-grandparents had to live through have had no effect on me.

As a result of the persecution, humiliation and fear my mother, Ruth Böhm, was subjected to both in Germany before the war and in Great Britain during and after the war, I believe that, for the rest of her life, she was left with low self-esteem and a recurring expectation that things would always go wrong for her. And of course they often did. Sadly, I have inherited these tendencies from my mother, and it would be no exaggeration to say that on many occasions in the past, this character flaw has caused me great despair and driven me to the very edge of my own sanity.

Therefore, if we believe, as I do, that one of the reasons for my mother's often flawed personality was her suffering in the aftermath of the Holocaust and that I am the way I am because I have inherited some aspects of her character, then in a sense, I am indeed also a victim of the Holocaust. I am convinced that the ripples of despair, agony and endless posing of the *'Why?'* question have trickled down from generation to generation and have, to a greater or lesser extent, affected all of us within this now dispersed yet still spiritually connected family.

As part of my quest to discover more about my own identity, I decided to have a sample of my DNA analysed, hoping that this might provide some empirical evidence as to who I really am. I had always considered myself to be Welsh, as Wales was where I was born and brought up, spent the first 20 years of my life, and even after having lived in Germany for the last 13 years, I still feel that I am going home each time I go back to this magical part of the United Kingdom. When the results of my DNA test came back, it was with some surprise and a certain element of shock that I read my personal ethnicity analysis:

European-Jewish 50%

Poland, Slovakia, Hungary & Moravia,

Germany, Netherlands, Belgium & Luxembourg

German-speaking middle Europe 10%

England, Wales and Southern England 38%

So there it was in black and white. At least 60 per cent of who I am is Jewish, Central European and German speaking, and only a little bit of me is actually Welsh, probably barely enough to even justify wearing a daffodil on St David's Day. It was now clear that I would have to re-evaluate my identity and sense of who I really am.

After receiving my DNA report, I now know that, genetically speaking at least, I stem mainly from Jewish middle-European, German-speaking stock. But what does this actually mean? If we believe what the science tells us, then it may indeed be the case that genes have an influence on character traits and that character traits help shape personality and, ultimately, a sense of our own identity. But does any of this actually have any effect on how we really see ourselves?

This book began with my mother, Ruth Böhm, standing in a railway station in Breslau in May 1939 about to leave her homeland forever, so it seems only fitting that I should return to the one person who gave me life to bring this story to a close because, in so many ways, I too have come full circle. I began life as the child of a Jewish, German-speaking immigrant woman in a drab Welsh mining town and embarked on a journey that was to last more than half a century. Unfortunately, it cannot be said that my mother had a happy life or a long one. After being wrenched away from an idyllic existence in the bosom of a loving family only to be arrested and imprisoned in the very country that was meant to offer her refuge, she made her way through life as best she could. But her stubbornness and pride often led her to make many bad decisions, and in some ways, she became her own worst enemy.

After just ten years, her marriage to George ended in failure, but in 1966, when my father died, Ruth slipped effortlessly into the role of the 'merry widow' as if it had been created just for her. Above all, she loved socializing with friends, dancing, baking cakes, being close to the sea, laughing and simply having fun. She had many good friends and, during the last ten years of her life, had a succession of boyfriends, most of whom were very good to her. When I was younger, she would sometimes lapse into a reflective and nostalgic mood and, with a sigh and sadness in her voice, would simply say, 'I deserve a better life than this.' And my mother did indeed deserve a better life than the one she had, and even today, I feel a deep sense of sorrow when I think about how different her life could have been had she lived longer. She had reconnected with her sister, Ilse, just a year before she died, and I am convinced that the two of them would have become close again and that my mother would eventually have gone to Australia to at last be reunited with the family she had lost so tragically many years before.

Ruth Böhm 1957

As with any journey, it is not so much the destination which is important but rather the various stopping-off places along the way because these staging posts often give the traveller a clue as to which way to go next. As I now look back over my 69 years of life, I can see many of these staging posts slowly emerging from the mist of the past to show me clearly where I have travelled on my journey, where I took a correct turn and where I took a wrong fork in the road. I see an unhappy childhood and mediocre performance at school. I see loneliness and a deep sense of not belonging, and I see a yearning to escape my broken home and dysfunctional family. I see the unexpected luxury of a university education where I discovered the intricate beauty of the German language and the mind-expanding potential of philosophy. I see academic success despite a breakdown that was to spark a depression that would recur time and time again over many years. I see a succession of meaningless jobs that would ultimately launch me into the wrong career which however was to last for 25 years. I see numerous unsuccessful relationships with women, two failed marriages and many friendships lost because of my often self-destructive character flaws.

These then were what I would call the wrong turns, but there have also been times during my journey at which I have chosen the right path. I have two wonderful children whom I am immensely proud of, and the years that I spent in Australia between 1988 and 1995 enabled me for the first time to build a relationship with my mother's extended family and to simply allow my 'Jewishness' to emerge. It quickly became clear to me during those early months in Australia that virtually all the living Australian descendants of Louis and Jenni Böhm were practicing Jews. This was something that was completely new for me. For the first time in my life, I donned the traditional *kippah* (brimless cap) before celebrating the important Jewish holidays such as Hanukkah and Pesach with my new family who warmly welcomed both me and my wife into their homes. Although I am not a religious person, those memorable occasions filled me with great pride, a sense of belonging and a deeply felt spirituality.

In Katscher, Louis and Jenni Böhm had lived at No. 3 Thrömerstrasse. In the world of the Tarot, the Angel Number 3 is said to represent 'growth, inspiration, inner guidance and manifestation'. This number is also believed to indicate that the universe is giving you all the support and guidance you need to fulfil your desires and life mission. Three has become my lucky number. I have discovered real fulfilment in my third career, teaching, and have also found true happiness, love and a sense of belonging with my third wife and absolute soul mate, Christine. Finally, I have found complete contentment and a new sense of purpose living in Germany, my third and final country of domicile.

On 12 April 2019, I finally completed my own circle of life by taking up German citizenship. Although the ceremony itself took no longer than 20 minutes, the immense significance of the occasion did not fail to escape me on that warm spring afternoon. I was fully aware that I had made a conscious decision to become a permanent citizen of the country that had been responsible for murdering several members of my own family.

On more than one occasion, I have been asked how it is possible for me to feel at home living in Germany given the tragic events that befell the Böhm family during the Hitler regime. I have spent many tortured hours grappling with this question, and although I have been unable to arrive at a definitive answer, three deeply held convictions have enabled me to make a kind of peace with my conscience. Firstly, I am and always will be part German, and as such, I have always had a close affinity with the country, its language, literature, music and culture. Secondly, Germany today bears no resemblance to the country that enabled Adolf Hitler's meteoric rise to power in 1933. The Germany that I know and have come to love is a tolerant, peaceful and caring nation and is undoubtedly one of the most multicultural societies in the world today. Chancellor Angela Merkel's much-criticized decision in 2015 to allow more than a million refugees to settle in Germany and build new lives for themselves and their families will, I believe, go down in history as a completely unselfish act of humanity by a country willing to extend the hand of friendship to the thousands of decent people forced to flee their homes in the many war-torn regions of the world. Thirdly, whether or not we believe in a god, forgiveness is something we are all capable of and yet is still sadly lacking in the world today.

The many conversations I have had with German people over the years about Adolf Hitler and the Holocaust have made me realise that there is a collective sense of guilt in this country about its past. This guilt permeates the national consciousness like a stain that is almost impossible to remove. But I truly believe that there is only one way to render this stain invisible, and that is for the world to find a way to forgive Germany and the Germans for the horrific events that took place on its soil more than 70 years ago. For my part, I know within my heart that I have forgiven Germany for the tragedy and indescribable suffering it unleashed on the Böhm family during what was undoubtedly the blackest period in modern European history.

Reconstructing the complex and often tragic story of Louis and Jenni Böhm and the family they created has been an immensely rewarding and illuminating experience for me, and it has truly helped me discover who I really am – a British-born, German-speaking European with strong Jewish roots and heritage who has settled permanently in the country of his ancestors. In part at least, I owe this new sense of identity and belonging to Louis and Jenni Böhm, and for this I pay tribute to them because I have finally come home.

ACKNOWLEDGMENTS

This book would not have been possible without the help of many different individuals. First of all, I would like to thank those members of the extended Böhm family who kindly made available to me an absolute treasure trove of letters, photographs, documents and personal anecdotes, all of which greatly helped to bring the book to life: Peter Vincent, Dennis Levy, Susan Levy, Stephen Freeman, Susan Ray, Jenni Böhm, Ron Hirsch and Katryn van Dyck.

I would also like to thank the Szwej family in Kietrz from the bottom of my heart for their generous hospitality in allowing Lucy and I to spend a memorable day inside Louis and Jenni's former home, for showing us around Kietrz and for allowing me to include photos of her family and their house in the book.

A big thank you must also go to Heniek Huss and Stanislawa Rychlik, my Polish/German sleuths on the ground in Silesia who, over the past two years, have sent me numerous newspaper articles and factual documentation relating to Katscher and the Böhm family in the pre-war era.

I would like to thank the very talented Jack Bedford for doing such a great job on the layout of the preliminary version of the book.

I owe a great debt of gratitude to my late mother-in-law, Christa Vogel, who devoted many hours of her own time helping me to decipher dozens of letters written in old German Sütterlin script. As we painstakingly translated the letters, she became completely engrossed in the unfolding story of the Böhms and would, I am sure, have loved to read the finished book. Sadly, this was not to be as she died suddenly, just months before I finished the final draft. Her son-in-law, Ingo Busch, kindly stepped in to help me translate those letters that Christa had been unable to complete.

Finally, I must of course thank my wife, Christine, for all her moral support, encouragement and good advice over the past three years and for never allowing me to give up on the project, even though there were certainly times when that was all I wanted do.

REFERENCES

I think it is fair to say that without the help of the internet, this book would never have seen the light of day. The vast amount of information and resources now available online for those people with enough time and patience on their hands is truly staggering.

By identifying and accessing countless genealogy sites, online databases, university libraries, Holocaust memorial sites, books and historical resources websites, my task of reconstructing the Böhm story was made significantly easier. I would therefore like to acknowledge the following sources that I found to be particularly helpful during my research:

Ancestry.com and Ancestry.de

Urzad Miejski w Kietrzu (registry office in Katscher)

Oppeln State Archives

http://opole.ap.gov.pl/resources/resources-characteristics.html

Arolsen Digital Archives, Germany

https://arolsen-archives.org/

Leobschütz historical website

https://www.leobschütz-oberschlesien.de

United States Holocaust Memorial Museum

https://www.ushmm.org/

Czech Republic Holocaust database

https://www.holocaust.cz

Virtual Schtetl

https://www.Sztetl.org.pl

JewishGen.org

https://www.jewishgen.org/databases/

Polska na fotografii

www.Fotopolska.Eu

Verein für Computergenealogie

Yad Vashem Holocaust database, Louis Böhm entry: https://yvng.yadvashem.org/nameDetails.html?language=en&itemId=11478109&ind=1

Breslau (Wroclaw) – Alte Strassennamen

Helen Fry, *Freud's War* - The History Press Ltd; Illustrated Edition (1 January 2009)

Fred Pelican, *From Dachau to Dunkirk* - Vallentine Mitchell, February 1993

Ernest Heppner, USHMM Oral History, 1999

BBC WW2, the 'People's War' page

Willy Cohn, *No Justice in Germany: The Breslau Diaries, 1933–1941* - Stanford University Press 2012

Eva Neisser Echenberg, *Walter's Welcome* - Skyhorse 2018

AMSTERDAM PUBLISHERS HOLOCAUST LIBRARY

The series **Holocaust Survivor Memoirs World War II** consists of the following autobiographies of survivors:

Outcry. Holocaust Memoirs, by Manny Steinberg

Hank Brodt Holocaust Memoirs. A Candle and a Promise, by Deborah Donnelly

The Dead Years. Holocaust Memoirs, by Joseph Schupack

Rescued from the Ashes. The Diary of Leokadia Schmidt, Survivor of the Warsaw Ghetto, by Leokadia Schmidt

My Lvov. Holocaust Memoir of a twelve-year-old Girl, by Janina Hescheles

Remembering Ravensbrück. From Holocaust to Healing, by Natalie Hess

Wolf. A Story of Hate, by Zeev Scheinwald with Ella Scheinwald

Save my Children. An Astonishing Tale of Survival and its Unlikely Hero, by Leon Kleiner with Edwin Stepp

Holocaust Memoirs of a Bergen-Belsen Survivor & Classmate of Anne Frank, by Nanette Blitz Konig

Defiant German - Defiant Jew. A Holocaust Memoir from inside the Third Reich, by Walter Leopold with Les Leopold

In a Land of Forest and Darkness. The Holocaust Story of two Jewish Partisans, by Sara Lustigman Omelinski

Holocaust Memories. Annihilation and Survival in Slovakia, by Paul Davidovits

From Auschwitz with Love. The Inspiring Memoir of Two Sisters' Survival, Devotion and Triumph Told by Manci Grunberger Beran & Ruth Grunberger Mermelstein, by Daniel Seymour

Remetz. Resistance Fighter and Survivor of the Warsaw Ghetto, by Jan Yohay Remetz

My March Through Hell. A Young Girl's Terrifying Journey to Survival, by Halina Kleiner with Edwin Stepp

* * *

The series **Holocaust Survivor True Stories WWII** consists of the following biographies:

Among the Reeds. The true story of how a family survived the Holocaust, by Tammy Bottner

A Holocaust Memoir of Love & Resilience. Mama's Survival from Lithuania to America, by Ettie Zilber

Living among the Dead. My Grandmother's Holocaust Survival Story of Love and Strength, by Adena Bernstein Astrowsky

Heart Songs. A Holocaust Memoir, by Barbara Gilford

Shoes of the Shoah. The Tomorrow of Yesterday, by Dorothy Pierce

Hidden in Berlin. A Holocaust Memoir, by Evelyn Joseph Grossman

Separated Together. The Incredible True WWII Story of Soulmates Stranded an Ocean Apart, by Kenneth P. Price, Ph.D.

The Man Across the River. The incredible story of one man's will to survive the Holocaust, by Zvi Wiesenfeld

If Anyone Calls, Tell Them I Died. A Memoir, by Emanuel (Manu) Rosen

The House on Thrömerstrasse. A Story of Rebirth and Renewal in the Wake of the Holocaust, by Ron Vincent

Dancing with my Father. His hidden past. Her quest for truth. How Nazi Vienna shaped a family's identity, by Jo Sorochinsky

The Story Keeper. Weaving the Threads of Time and Memory - A Memoir, by Fred Feldman

Krisia's Silence. The Girl who was not on Schindler's List, by Ronny Hein

Defying Death on the Danube. A Holocaust Survival Story, by Debbie J. Callahan with Henry Stern

A Doorway to Heroism. A decorated German-Jewish Soldier who became an American Hero, by Rabbi W. Jack Romberg

The Shoemaker's Son. The Life of a Holocaust Resister, by Laura Beth Bakst

The Redhead of Auschwitz. A True Story, by Nechama Birnbaum

Land of Many Bridges. My Father's Story, by Bela Ruth Samuel Tenenholtz

Creating Beauty from the Abyss. The Amazing Story of Sam Herciger, Auschwitz Survivor and Artist, by Lesley Ann Richardson

On Sunny Days We Sang. A Holocaust Story of Survival and Resilience, by Jeannette Grunhaus de Gelman

Painful Joy. A Holocaust Family Memoir, by Max J. Friedman

I Give You My Heart. A True Story of Courage and Survival, by Wendy Holden

Monsters and Miracles. Horror, Heroes and the Holocaust, by Ira Wesley Kitmacher

Flower of Vlora. Growing up Jewish in Communist Albania, by Anna Kohen

Zaidy's War, by Martin Bodek

In the Time of Madmen, by Mark A. Prelas

* * *

The series **Jewish Children in the Holocaust** consists of the following autobiographies of Jewish children hidden during WWII in the Netherlands:

Searching for Home. The Impact of WWII on a Hidden Child, by Joseph Gosler

See You Tonight and Promise to be a Good Boy! War memories, by Salo Muller

Sounds from Silence. Reflections of a Child Holocaust Survivor, Psychiatrist and Teacher, by Robert Krell

Sabine's Odyssey. A Hidden Child and her Dutch Rescuers, by Agnes Schipper

The Journey of a Hidden Child, by Harry Pila with Robin Black

* * *

The series **New Jewish Fiction** consists of the following novels, written by Jewish authors. All novels are set in the time during or after the

Holocaust.

The Corset Maker. A Novel, by Annette Libeskind Berkovits

Escaping the Whale. The Holocaust is over. But is it ever over for the next generation? by Ruth Rotkowitz

When the Music Stopped. Willy Rosen's Holocaust, by Casey Hayes

Hands of Gold. One Man's Quest to Find the Silver Lining in Misfortune, by Roni Robbins

There was a garden in Nuremberg. A Novel, by Navina Michal Clemerson

Aftermath: Coming-of-Age on Three Continents, by Annette Libeskind Berkovits

The Girl Who Counted Numbers. A Novel, by Roslyn Bernstein

The Butterfly and the Axe, by Omer Bartov

* * *

The series **Holocaust Books for Young Adults** consists of the following novels, based on true stories:

On the Run. A True Story, by Suzette Sheft

The Boy behind the Door. How Salomon Kool Escaped the Nazis, by David Tabatsky

The Precious Few. An Inspirational Saga of Courage based on True Stories, by David Twain with Art Twain

Want to be an AP book reviewer?

Reviews are very important in a world dominated by the social media and social proof. Please drop us a line if you want to join the *AP review team*. We will then add you to our list of advance reviewers. No strings attached, and we promise that we will not be spamming you.

info@amsterdampublishers.com

www.ingramcontent.com/pod-product-compliance
Lightning Source LLC
La Vergne TN
LVHW020431070526
838199LV00026B/599/J